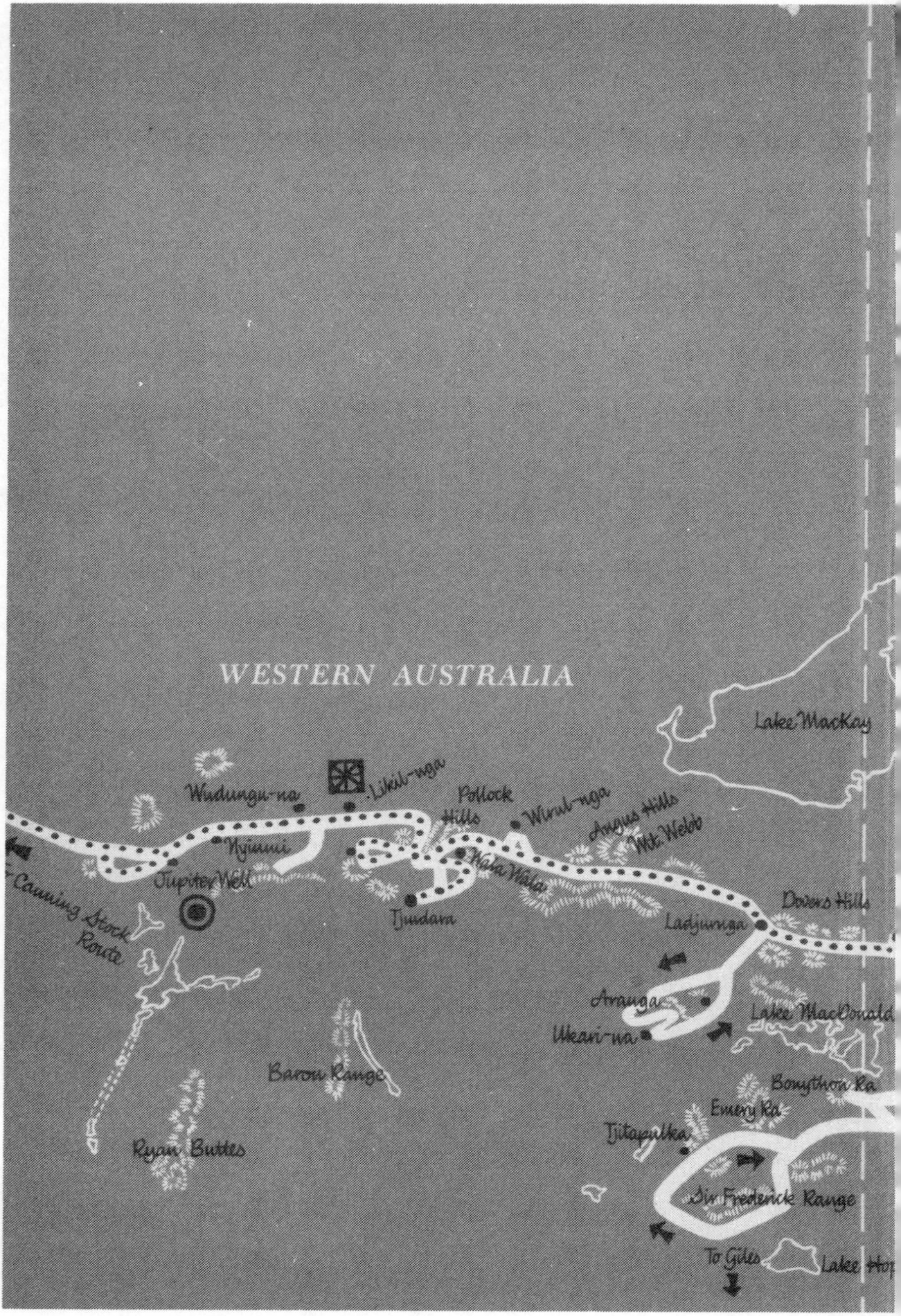

WESTERN AUSTRALIA
Lake MacKay
Wudungu-na
Likil-nga
Pollock Hills
Wirul-nga
Angus Hills
Mt. Webb
Njimni
Jupiter Well
Wala Wala
Canning Stock Route
Tjudara
Dovers Hills
Ladjunga
Arunga
Ukari-na
Lake MacDonald
Baron Range
Boughton Ra
Emery Ra
Tjitapulka
Ryan Buttes
Sir Frederick Range
To Giles

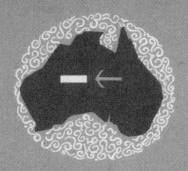

Sketch Map
Showing Route of Pintubi Patrol 1963

Lockwood's Patrol with J. P. Long indicated thus

J. P. Long's Second Patrol

Wili Waterhole where we found Jugudi and family

Wudungu Waterhole where we found Anatjari and family

Jupiter Well where we found Yaliti and his family group

NORTHERN TERRITORY

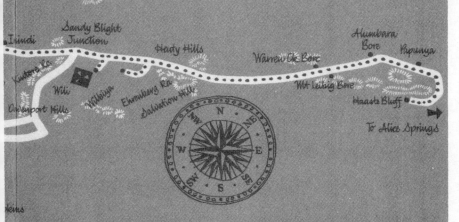

The Lizard Eaters

Douglas Lockwood

 J.B. BOOKS AUSTRALIA

Other books by Douglas Lockwood

Crocodiles and Other People
Fair Dinkum
Life on the Daly River (with Nancy Polishuk)
I, the Aboriginal
We, the Aborigines

This edition is an exclusive production published in 2006 for
J. B. Books
PO Box 118
Marleston 5033
South Australia
Phone/Fax (08) 8297 1669

First published in Australia in hardcover 1964
by Cassell Australia Ltd

Printed in Australia by McPherson's printing Group

National Library of Australia Cataloguing-in-Publication Data:

Lockwood, Douglas 1918–1980
        The lizard eaters

            ISBN 1 8602 644 4
            1. Pintupi (Australian People). 2. Aborigines, Australian – Social life
            and customs. I. Title.

305.89915

For Jeremy Long, Ted Evans
and Dr. John Hargrave, who were the first
to take aid to the Pintubi.
All three are still working
for the Aborigines.

Acknowledgement

I want to express my gratitude to the Northern Territory Director of Welfare, Mr. Harry Giese, for inviting me to accompany a government patrol to the Gibson Desert, thus making it possible for me to meet the remarkable Pintubi nomads in their natural environment.

I am grateful for the hospitality I was given by Mr and Mrs John Pender, at Haasts Bluff, and Mr and Mrs Alex Bishaw, at Yuendumu.

The enchantment of our desert journey was enriched by the comradeship of the men, European and Aboriginal, whose names appear in these pages. But it would not have been possible without the blessing of the Editors of The Herald and Weekly Times Ltd., Melbourne — my employers. I wrote a series of articles about the Pintubi which have already appeared in our newspapers.

DOUGLAS LOCKWOOD

Darwin,
1964.

THE LIZARD EATERS

The red horizon merges into sky
And shows the eye reality's a lie.
The lonely wind makes brown acacias sigh,
To tell the ear that silence, too, must die.

But can we speak of ear and eye out here?
Out here where sand and stillness vie? We can:
The eyes and ears of lizards, rats, in fear
Of eyes and ears of naked nomad man.

The sun makes sand, already red, red-hot,
As bare and lonely feet walk miles for mice,
For lizards, food, for water, life; and not
To find them means search on — so now, look twice.

With Thorny Devils, lizards on a string
The man returns to camp to sleep on sand,
To sleep and thirst, be pounded by the sting
Of cold night wind. This is his home, his land.

So life has been for many thousand years
An endless search for food and water; fears
There may not be a meal today; no tears
When hunter comes with nothing: death soon nears.

Contents

Illustrations

THE LIZARD EATERS

The Fringe Dwellers

Two young aboriginal boys attend school at Papunya settlement, one hundred and sixty miles west of Alice Springs in the arid heartland of Australia. They are neatly dressed. Their hair is combed. Their faces and hands are clean.

They are Yariari and Kanditjara, both aged twelve, of the Pintubi tribe. They have tribal brothers and sisters in the same classroom, where they are being taught to read and write English as a foreign language by Adrian Luck, a man who finds his environment of red desert and primitive black people far removed from the soft greens and blues and the sophisticated white students he knew in his early days as a teacher.

Other tribal relatives of Yariari and Kanditjara attend school at the Yuendumu settlement, about ninety miles north of Papunya. At both places there are mixtures of predominantly Pintubi and Wailbri tribesmen, but there are also small groups of Aranda, Pitjantjara, Loritja, Anmatjira and Kukutja people.

At first glance it may appear not unusual that Yariari, Kanditjara and their relatives should be at school. After all, nearly three thousand aboriginal children are receiving education in more than thirty specially staffed schools throughout the Northern Territory. This is assisting their integration in the European community more than any other single factor. The time is not far distant when trained

aboriginal teachers and artisans will take their place along-
side white Australians.

Nevertheless, the fact that Yariari and Kanditjara are at
school is not only unusual; it is truly remarkable. For these
children and those at Yuendumu have tribal uncles and
aunts who have not yet left the Stone Age. They are nomads
who still eat goannas, lizards, mountain devils, rats, mice,
dingoes and wild cats in the desert of sandhills and spinifex
between five hundred and six hundred miles west of Alice
Springs, and east of the Canning stockroute in Western
Australia.

Their address is between 128° and 126° E. and between
24° and 22° S. They are all naked hunters. They live in
Australia but have never heard the word. The harshness of
their existence is almost beyond belief — and yet it is true.

Only seven years ago Yariari and Kanditjara existed in this
desert, too, eating rodents and lizards and not much else.
Today they eat bread and beef and fruit which their desert
relatives have never seen. Perhaps nowhere in the world is
there a comparable gap in the mode of living of such close
relatives.

In 1963 I was privileged to accompany a patrol from the
Welfare Branch of Northern Territory Administration on a
fortnight's visit to the Pintubi tribal country.

We went in four-wheel-drive vehicles to a point 570 miles
west of Alice Springs and 200 miles inside Western Australia.
The Branch's Senior Research Officer, Jeremy Long, led the
patrol. He is six feet five inches tall, and an Arts graduate of
Sydney University who has specialized in anthropology. This
was his fifth visit to the Pintubi. At a place called Jupiter
Well, only thirty miles from our most westerly penetration,
I congratulated myself on being one of a very select group of
white men ever to have been there. But I won't ever boast
about it too blatantly, for while there I discovered that I had

been beaten to it by a white woman. Long's beautiful wife, Frances, went with him on an earlier trip. For some days thereafter I suffered from a wounded pride.

However, the compensations for that injury were well worthwhile, for we found what might be called The Last of the Primitives, perhaps the world's last Stone Age people, living in small family groups of between five and eleven men, women and children. The barren desert they have chosen as home, in spinifex sandhills which have kept them hidden for generations, does not yield enough food or water to support tribes. Only groups of fewer than a dozen people can hope to hunt and survive. It is an area almost deserted by kangaroos. Miserable desert soaks and rockholes, sometimes fifty miles apart, give just enough water to sustain itinerant life; but, as in all deserts, many waterholes fail when they are most badly needed. I was not surprised to hear, fairly regularly, the word 'perish' on the lips of aboriginal guides and interpreters who accompanied us. The Gibson Desert can be as treacherous as the Sahara, and there have been human and animal bones around dry soaks to prove it. A man might survive while walking fifty miles in hot weather from one failing waterhole to the next; but getting back, or to another, when he arrives with swollen tongue and finds dry sand instead of cool water is a different matter altogether.

Yet it was not the manner of the Pintubi's survival but the very fact of it that astonished me. I have lived and worked among aborigines in the Northern Territory for twenty years, regularly visiting remote outposts where man's advancement from earliest times is perceptible but not pronounced. It has been commonplace to find aboriginal people who make fire by rubbing sticks together and hunt their food with boomerangs, spears and stealth. I have grown accustomed to bearded men with matted hair, and women who give birth in the bush, without medical aid, as women did when human

beings first stood upright. Hundreds of these near primitives
are fringe-dwellers of our society at government settlements
and mission stations today. At Papunya and Yuendumu, at
Hooker Creek and Balgo Hills on the northern arc of the
desert ring, and Warburton Mission in the south, they are
cared for in such a way that the tribes, at long last, are once
again increasing.

Nevertheless, I had no conception that such primitiveness
as that of the Gibson Desert Pintubi remained on earth.
Adam and Eve must have lived like this in the Garden of
Eden; but at least they had a garden which, if you believe
your mythology, was rich in apples and serpents. The Pintubi
desert is far from being a garden. Only the hardiest plants —
spinifex, mulga, ti-tree and desert oaks — survive.

Most of the twenty-three people we found had not seen
white men before. I was privileged to be first to greet one
such tribesman and his family. This was truly a thrilling
experience and one I shall not forget.

Except for one or two pubic cloths among the women,
they had never worn clothing of any kind. The cloths had
apparently been acquired from tribesmen in contact with the
outside world. They had never bathed, never slept under a
blanket even though temperatures fall below freezing point,
and never eaten food other than lizards, goannas, rodents,
berries ground into a meal, fungi, an occasional euro, an
occasional dingo, and an occasional wild cat. These are the
only animals that can hope to survive in the almost waterless
sand country; yet how they exist while competing for a drink
with hungry hunters sitting on the waterholes is an equally
baffling mystery. I was not surprised to find that the surviv
ing wild life is that which, predominantly, can live without
water for long periods and, in some cases, altogether. Dogs
and cats must drink, though euros and reptiles may exist

without it. In spite of that, we saw the tracks of more wild dogs and cats than of any other form of life.

This, then, was the type of country and the kind of life that Yariari and Kanditjara left behind when they went with their parents and about two hundred other Pintubi to live, to learn, and to eat well at Papunya, Yuendumu, Balgo Hills and Warburton Mission. The wonder is not that they left when they did, when word filtered through that a new and secure life was promised at the settlements and missions; it is not that they survived for as long as they did — for perhaps fifteen thousand years since the aborigines first arrived in Australia; the real wonder is that when the desert began to be deserted there were a few hardy souls who elected to remain, who shunned the world they had heard of but not seen, and continued to eat lizards and dogs.

These were the remnants of humanity that we found; men, women and children who were in this world but not of it; tribal people separated from civilization by only a few hundred miles — and yet by thousands of years. That it should have been my good fortune to be one of a party which first made contact with them will remain with me always as one of the most exciting episodes of my career in the Australian outback.

The man I first greeted, the black man for whom I was the first white man, was named Anatjari. Like many tribal aborigines he is polygamous, supporting two wives, three small children, and a fourteen-year-old 'skin' brother in country where anyone but an expert hunter would quickly perish.

He came to us straight from the Stone Age, a man who, in caricature, would have carried a club and dragged women by the hair to his cave. He had no implements or weapons other than spears and knives he made from wood and stone. He did not have a plate, a cup, a knife or a fork. He drank from a shaped wooden pitchi — gritty water which came from a hole ten feet deep in the desert floor between ranges of sandhills. His children, until they could walk, were carried by their mothers. He was entirely naked but wore a grass string around his waist to carry lizards and any other game he might be lucky enough to catch.

Anatjari was made nervous and perhaps a little frightened by our arrival. His young son ran away after one quick look at us, but later returned. So did two tame dingoes he hunts and sleeps with.

These people had never seen running water, a tap, a tin of food, a building of any kind, a cow or a horse. But they had seen aeroplanes over their land infrequently — inexplicable phenomena they thought might be flying devils. When that happened they 'planted' themselves among clumps of spinifex and sometimes even buried themselves in the sand.

Apart from his spears, his digging sticks, his wooden vessels, his wives and his children, Anatjari had nothing else in the world. Nothing at all.

I little thought when I met him that there could be still more primitive people. Yet such was the case, for a few days later a man named Yaliti made Anatjari look almost sophisticated.

I first met Pintubi tribesmen at Papunya settlement, where about seven hundred aborigines are cared for by the government. Its existence is a tribute to the adaptability of the Wailbri and Pintubi tribes. Although the population is now bigger than on any other settlement in the Northern Territory, work on it began only in 1956 and occupation came three years later. Papunya grew from the official policy towards aboriginal welfare which recognized that before the nomadic people of the remote regions could make any progress towards a life within the Australian community social training would have to be undertaken on a scale previously not attempted or envisaged.

A site was selected north of the Haasts Bluff range and about thirty miles from the ration depot there. Water bores were sunk, an airstrip built, and construction begun on a complex of buildings to house administrative and technical staff. Papunya is now a small town. Including its aboriginal population it is, in fact, the sixth largest town in The Territory, with its own streets and street lights, a school, a hospital, a church, a canteen-store, and a dozen or more houses for the European workers.

The aborigines themselves still live in the open or in crude camps which are a blot on the landscape. However, a start has been made on prefabricated aluminium and concrete houses for suitable families and I have no doubt that future generations of these people will live as we do. This cannot be expected of the majority of the present adult population, who are only one stage removed from their former status of nomadic hunters. They are socially backward, and hidden behind a barrier of language which makes personal contact with Europeans difficult. Their progress towards acceptance of our standards in everything from hygiene to four walls and a roof will necessarily be slow, and will then be achieved only through education of the children. For the adults, it is already too late; you cannot teach an old tribesman to use a knife and fork when his fingers are patently less trouble and not associated, in his mind, with the spread of disease.

I would like to digress just a little further to discuss the immensity of the task facing Welfare officers in assimilating these people and their relatives — the primitives we met in the Gibson Desert who must soon be brought into closer contact with civilization if they are to be saved from dying out altogether.

The Wailbri and Pintubi at Papunya and Yuendumu are still strongly influenced by tribal law. The Welfare Branch acknowledges that the aborigines regard the area occupied by these settlements as part of their ancestral lands. They are still semi-nomadic, a fact designed to frustrate even the most patient teachers by interruption to the continuity of lessons.

Field workers are confronted by a complexity of pressing problems. The Wailbri and Pintubi adults and children speak no English. The teachers know that they must give inordinate attention to it in school, at the expense of other subjects. For until the aborigines understand English they cannot be expected to understand the ways of civilized men. Among the more primitive men and women there is opposition to subversion of the children to European ways of life because it leads to conflict with tribal law and has an unsettling effect on the children.

Few of the people living at Papunya and Yuendumu have seen any European society. They cannot therefore be expected to understand the incentives which activate Europeans in economic matters. The majority have been in contact with white society for a very short time indeed; people who have never lived with a roof over their heads are still arriving.

The concepts of work and competition are quite foreign to aboriginal thought. They have no application to a nomadic system of life. To men who have hunted and eaten all their food as soon as it is caught the idea of making provision for the future is incomprehensible.

One should not be surprised, therefore, that the officers of the Welfare Branch grappling with this situation see no easy or quick solution to the many problems inherent in the social transformation being attempted.

This was the situation at Papunya when I arrived and met Pintubi people who had been out of the desert for varying periods from thirty years to a few days. In the first group there was a diverting man named Junkata of the Juburula 'skin'. (The Pintubi and Wailbri tribes have eight common sub-sections: Jabaljari, Jagamara, Juburula, Jungarai, Jamba-jimba, Jabangadi, Jangala and Jabananga. The female sub-sections are identical except that each begins with 'N' instead of 'J'. Marriage and association within these skin-groups is strictly controlled.) Junkata is known throughout Central Australia as Nosepeg. He left the Gibson Desert near Lake MacDonald as a young man for the security offered at Hermannsburg Lutheran Mission station on the Finke River. Later he went to Haasts Bluff and, when it was established, to Papunya. He is a man of considerable influence among the Pintubi. He was to be our interpreter and one of our guides on the long journey to the sunset country. I shall write about him often, for he was a truly delightful companion and invaluable to the success of our expedition.

Nosepeg was present as interpreter when I interviewed Gunia Jugurba Jabaljari, Wadi Jugurba Jungarai and Jalyuri Jabaljari in their camp on the fringes of the settlement. Jalyuri had made a number of trips to Papunya from the desert country and was to be one of our guides. Gunia and Wadi were recent arrivals and still far from accustomed to their new environment. All three men had extremely soft and finely-boned faces, in contrast with the heavy, some-times coarse, features of the Wailbri. The word 'soft' applied especially to Gunia; his face was almost effeminate, and yet there was about him an unmistakable masculinity. In ancient

Greece he might have been regarded as a man of outstanding beauty.

Gunia, Wadi and Jalyuri spoke softly when they answered questions I asked them through Nosepeg. Wadi spoke in whispers, barely moving his lips, probably because in the desert there is no noise to compete with — and because they are professional hunters who do not make unnecessary sounds. It is too long between meals out there to have game disturbed by human voices. If he could answer a question by sign-talk, without speaking at all, he invariably did so. This, I discovered, was a trait common to all the Pintubi nomads.

It was from them that I first heard of the tribesmen's fear of the aeroplanes which occasionally flew over their country on the way to and from other worlds they did not know about. Gunia, Wadi and Jalyuri had each hidden under spinifex bushes when the planes appeared. It should be remembered that the other name for spinifex is Porcupine Grass, whose needle points can pierce the toughest skin. Burrowing beneath it would not be fun, especially as none of these men wore clothing. The worst period of their lives in this respect occurred between May and October in 1953 when about three hundred sorties were flown over the desert by Mosquito aircraft from No. 87 (P/R) Squadron, R.A.A.F., led by Squadron-Leader (now Wing-Commander) C. D. Browne. These planes flew at twenty-five thousand feet while taking aerial photographs for a national mapping project. At that height they would be barely visible, which may have added to the fear caused by the constant roar of their engines.

Gunia and Wadi had one day of another terror — one which still obviously affected them when they spoke about it. The first motor vehicle they had seen was a road grader in the charge of Len Beadell, of the Federal Department of Supply, who was grading a track across the desert to link

Alice Springs with the Canning stockroute, Wiluna, and eventually Perth, fifteen hundred miles away. To nomadic tribesmen who had never seen a vehicle of any kind, that grader was like a huge dinosaur coming after them through the sandhills, roaring and belching smoke and dust as it bit the red earth with its great mouth of steel, and pawed it with circular legs.

Nosepeg questioned them and explained graphically that they were terrified. They ran for their lives, streaking across the dunes, never lighting a fire which might betray their whereabouts, and remaining hidden for weeks. When they eventually returned the monstrous contraption had gone, and they were glad. But the immense track was there as a constant reminder of the devil that had passed: the imprint of huge tractor tyres and the endless 'road' bitten from the desert floor. They approached it while quaking with fear, afraid lest the tracks themselves should spring up to devour them. For none of these men had seen the track of anything bigger than a kangaroo.

A forecast of the harsh life in the desert that I was later to see was given by Wadi and Gunia, who matter-of-factly said they often went for two days and sometimes longer without food and were permanently hungry. Regular meal times were unheard of, and regular meals rare. In spite of that, I assumed that when they ate there was plenty to eat. Little did I realize then that a meal for five or six Pintubi might consist of a shared goanna or a handful of Mountain Devils — a small, spiked lizard weighing not more than a few ounces. I shall not quickly forget my first sight of a three-year-old aboriginal girl cooking her own small lizard in her own fire, extracting the entrails with her tiny fingers, and then eating her way along it from stem to stern. The entire operation took less than five minutes, for the reptile measured not more than six inches. Nor did I understand

until I saw for myself what meagre supply these desert
people meant when they spoke of water. I imagined that
somewhere in the desert we would find big natural springs.
One such waterhole, known as Vaughan Springs, is the pride
of Mount Doreen cattle station, near the eastern extremity
of the desert. And the map of this country is liberally
shaded with areas of blue marked Lake MacDonald, Lake
Mackay, Lake Hopkins, Lake Wills, Lake Hazlett and Lake
White. When I refer to these places in the following pages,
however, the reader should supply his own inverted commas.
Lake MacDonald is really 'lake' MacDonald, and so are the
rest of them. They are nothing more than dry salt pans. Why
they have been designated as lakes, giving an entirely false
picture of the country to anyone who hasn't been there, is
a mystery.

Talking about water led me to ask Gunia, Wadi and
Jalyuri about the sea. They had never heard of it. I asked
about fish. They did not understand. I tried to describe
sharks and whales. But how can a man who has never seen
a mullet believe that creatures as big as houses live in the
sea? The tax on his imagination is more demanding still
when it is realized that he has seen his first house of any
kind — the iron roofs of Papunya — only a few days earlier.

I put some silver coins in Gunia's hand. He held them up
to examine but they meant nothing to him. When Nosepeg
explained that they were money which could be exchanged
for flour, tea and sugar at the canteen his eyes lit up beautifully. He looked at them again and slowly put them in the
pocket of his tattered trousers, fingering them constantly,
perhaps in case they burnt a hole there.

Gunia had been at Papunya, away from his desert home,
for only a few days. He had still not settled down sufficiently
to visit the canteen to see, for the first time, purchases being
made by more sophisticated men and women with pounds,

shillings and pence. That day was to come; it would be, for him, like the first visit of a country bumpkin to a city emporium. Nevertheless, Gunia knew what it was, when Nosepeg told him, that the money would buy. He had eaten damper made with white man's flour, and drunk tea sweetened with sugar. He saw the others carrying it in bags and may have wondered if, one day, he might himself own a bag of flour, a bag of sugar, and a packet of tea. He was already about twenty-five years old. I thought of him as a truly primitive man until, less than a week later, I met a man who, when I gave him money, did not know what Nosepeg was talking about when told that it would buy flour, sugar and tea. He tasted each of these things for the first time when we produced them that night.

Wadi was a married man with two wives and one child. Although he left the desert with Gunia and had been at Papunya only a few days, he had already visited the canteen. I talked to him for a long time, trying to find out from his monosyllables and signs, interpreted by Nosepeg, what he thought of the new world.

He was diffident and perplexed. I could learn little from his speech, but it wasn't difficult to read his face and his eyes and to observe his manner. And I was convinced that he still suffered from shock at discovering a world he hadn't known existed. That conviction was to be reinforced dramatically a fortnight later when we returned from the desert ourselves with two brand new initiates to civilization and I was able to watch their reaction at first hand.

Gunia, Wadi and Jalyuri were still nomads and hunters and always would be in their hearts, even though they became fringe dwellers at Papunya. But their children would grow up as sophisticated human beings, schooled like Yariari and Kanditjara in English and arithmetic, able to read and to count and to express abstract thoughts quite beyond the

comprehension of their parents. Wherever I went among
these people, whether at Papunya or Yuendumu, I found
that, generally, it was for the sake of the children that they
had left their tribal ground, the desert country that had
miraculously supported them for centuries. At Yuendumu I
met a group of eleven Pintubi men who went there soon after
their first contact. They were met by a Welfare Branch patrol
led by Mr E. C. Evans near Lake Mackay in 1957. Two of
them, Patuta Jabanunga and Kirapi Juburula (Arthur and
Jim) made it clear that although they liked living close to
the unlimited supplies of water and food at Yuendumu, they
would return to their country except that they wanted their
children to be educated. They had seen the benefits that
education gave to other aborigines, and they wanted it for
their own children. The price was exile — exile, to be sure,
from a harsh and pitiless land, but the place they individu-
ally called My Country. Few people who are not aborigines
themselves can understand the depth of feeling in an aboriginal's heart when he talks about his ancestral land.

The hunters' instinct is with these people always. If I
needed any proof of this it was provided on the day I sat
talking to Gunia, Wadi and Jalyuri at Papunya. They listened
intently as Nosepeg translated one of my questions. Then a
bird chirped. Instantly they were alert and crouching, their
hands groping automatically for spears or throwing sticks
they didn't have. In a moment they realized they were in a
place where food was provided and relaxed, but not before
betraying the thought always uppermost in the mind of the
hunter: food for survival.

The suffering of the Pintubi in sickness, accident and
death, quite apart from their daily fight for survival, can only
be imagined. Yet my imagination was stirred when I saw
young children whose bellies were ballooned in advanced

stages of malnutrition. I saw a young boy who could not walk and had to crawl because he was badly infected with yaws.

Nevertheless, such suffering is comparatively slight against the agonies which must have tormented three particular men.

The first of these is Wadi Jugruba of the Jambajimba skin. He lives at Yuendumu and is known there as Peg-Leg Mick. He was found in the Lake Mackay region by the Evans Expedition in 1957. Jeremy Long, our present leader, was a member of that party. Mick was a physically normal man except that his right leg was off just below the knee. Yet he had never seen a white man and there are no skilled surgeons among the Pintubi. How, then, was his leg amputated?

When I spoke to Mick there was Christ-like suffering in his eyes. Here was a man who had been through agony that defied description. He spoke little — it almost seemed that he had been stricken dumb by suffering — and I had to get his story from another man.

As a young man, Mick sustained a spear wound in a tribal fight. I could not be sure what the fight was about, although I'd be surprised if women weren't at the bottom of it, for they are notorious trouble-makers in the tribes as well as in more sophisticated salons. Mick's wound became infected and gangrenous and for four months he groaned in agony. Food and water were so short that his horde had to keep moving around the desert or perish. Mick, obviously, could not walk, so Patuta Jabanunga, the man known at Yuendumu as Arthur, carried him during this entire period while they hunted and walked, sometimes thirty or forty miles a day. The alternative was that Mick should be abandoned and allowed to perish, for a horde which might be a hundred miles away in a week could not hope to send messengers back with food and water. It must have been a grim occasion when his naked relatives sat down and deliberated on what

was to be done. The arguments for life and death pro-
pounded at that conference are never likely to be known
although, in the stern tradition of the tribes, there would
certainly have been advocates for his abandonment. That
was something Patuta was not prepared to accept. The
alternative was to carry him, and the man who did the
carrying would be the man who suggested it — his potential,
and later actual, father-in-law. He had a tribal obligation to
care for him.

And so this remarkable man survived.

I questioned them closely as to the ultimate method of
amputation, and was assured repeatedly that cutting had
been unnecessary. Perhaps that was just as well, because the
implements these people possessed were made exclusively of
wood and stone. The leg, I was told, finally fell off when the
flesh had withered and the bone been eaten through. The
stub was packed in mud made with a little of their precious
water and healed splendidly. I shall not blame any reader
who regards this story as being beyond the bounds of
credibility. However, his photograph is in this book.

Not the least astonishing aspect of Mick's recovery is that
today he walks with the aid of a long pole and can move
as fast as a man with two good legs. He uses it as a pole-
vaulter might, stepping out across the land with giant strides.
Shortly after his contact with white men Mick and other
Pintubi walked from the tribal country around Lake Mackay
and in thirteen days reached Mount Doreen station, about
one hundred and fifty miles away. They hunted their food
on the way.

The second story of suffering concerns Ngugudi Tjipula
of the Juburula skin, Nosepeg's tribal brother, who has only
one arm. In spite of this handicap, Ngugudi came with us
from Papunya as a guide and would have stayed with us to
the end of the journey except that one of our vehicles broke

down on the third day out and had to be abandoned. That meant dividing our load, both of men and materials, and Ngugudi was one who had to be sent back by Jeremy Long.

In the early nineteen fifties Ngugudi walked out of the desert to seek a more secure way of life at the Lutheran mission outpost at Haasts Bluff. Soon afterwards he was detained by police as a witness in a tribal murder. Ngugudi himself had committed no offence, but to prevent him running away from the legal trouble about to follow he was handcuffed to another man and chained to a tree. Ngugudi, a desert man with only brief contact, was terrified. He worked on the chain all night with stones, and before dawn had managed to sever one of the links, and thus escaped. The bracelet, however, was still on his arm. Unfortunately it was of the ratchet type, and in his frantic attempt to loosen it, Ngugudi managed only to make it tighter — and still tighter. He was in the bush for many weeks, fearing the consequences of returning. But when infection set in and the pain became agonizing he was forced to do so. Even so, he was too late, and he had to be taken to Alice Springs hospital where the arm was amputated. Ngugudi has since become known in the district as Paddy Handcuffs, a fitting and permanent indictment of the cruelty and thoughtlessness which was commonplace in The Territory not so many years ago. Another man, Walter Talbulba, is known as Jaynajara — an aboriginal translation of 'chain carrier'. He is said to have spent a long period with the iron bonds of the law attached to him.

The third story of suffering is of a man who died from natural causes — but nature was cruel indeed. His name was Windaru, of the Jangala skin. Near a desert soak called Watulbu, he followed porcupine tracks into a cave, intending to catch it for his family's food. Windaru squeezed through a small aperture at the farthest extremity of the cave, which

ended in such a confined space that he could not turn
around. Nor could he force his buttocks back through the
hole which had admitted him. He died there, alone, on his
hands and knees.

These stories, however much they underlined the stoicism
of the Pintubi, were really incidental instances of individual
suffering. In the following weeks I was to learn that these
people suffered as a group, throughout their lives, from near-
starvation, intense cold from which they had no protection,
and intolerable summer heat in a land offering little shade.
Yet they were apparently unaware of suffering, for that was
their heritage.

Before passing on to the personal story of my journey a
few historical and other facts about the Pintubi and their
country may be of interest.

The earliest exploration of the area, although cursory,
occurred in 1873 when Colonel Egerton Warburton led an
expedition from Alice Springs to the Kimberleys in the north-
west of Western Australia. However, he passed well to the
north of Lake Mackay, which was not discovered until it was
seen from the air in 1930. In 1933 the Australian explorer,
Michael Terry, passed through the northern part of the
Pintubi tribal land while travelling to Tanami with camels.
He named many of the geographic features. Warburton's
journal makes frequent references to wild aborigines, sometimes described as 'the enemy'. I have no doubt that they
were Pintubi, although they must have been well to the
north of our track, which led us between Lake Mackay and
Lake MacDonald.

The Honourable David Carnegie passed to the west of
this area in 1897 while on his way from Hall's Creek to
Kalgoorlie. Carnegie made several trips by camels into the
eastern and northern interior of Western Australia. He

personally financed the 1896-97 expedition with his profits
from gold mining. On that journey he reached Hall's Creek
and found new auriferous country there. He returned to the
south along the eastern side of Lake MacDonald, then veer-
ing south-west through the Rawlinson Ranges. *Spinifex and
Sand*, a book he wrote about his journeys, was published two
years later. As we rode along in the comparative comfort of
four-wheel-drive vehicles, although still subject to fairly
severe spinal abrasions, I was conscious of how much easier
our trip must be; his was an ordeal, ours almost a conducted
tour. Even so, his was probably a sinecure by comparison
with Ernest Giles' trip — really the first penetration of the
Gibson Desert — in 1874. Giles named it after Alfred Gibson,
a young South Australian member of his party who disappeared while searching for water near the Alfred and
Marie Ranges, about a hundred miles south-west of our
position at Jupiter Well.

Warburton on his trip was forced by the absence of water
to remain in one part of the desert for fifty-six days. Exploration parties he sent out eventually found a small soak a
hundred miles from his base camp, and he was able to
replenish his supplies.

An occasional prospector may also have gone out with
camels, but it seems a remote possibility that any of them
would have reached the Western Australian border. The
legendary Lasseter, who died in a cave 200 miles further
south, was probably in Pintubi country. A pioneer pastoralist,
William Braitling, of Mount Doreen station, infrequently
visited the desert between his property and Lake Mackay.
Lutheran missionaries occasionally went out on camels from
Hermannsburg. But it was not until 1957 when the Evans
Expedition penetrated to Lake Mackay that regular contact
with the desert Pintubi began. Even then, the contact was
spasmodic and isolated. Our patrol was to show that family

groups still existed who had never seen white men, or been seen by them. Moreover, we were to learn of the existence of people we could not even find. At Yuendumu, Arthur Patuta Jabanunga told me that his brother, Mamutja, his three wives and several children, were living near Lake MacDonald. He asked us to bring them back; but Mamutja, wherever he was, did not answer our smoke signals. At least three other families also remained hidden.

However, patrols into the remotest corners of the Pintubi country are likely to be more frequent in future. I shall be surprised if any tribesmen who have not yet had contact remain at the end of two or three years. This has all been simplified by the work of the Gun Barrell Road Construction Company, led by Len Beadell, which has graded a track across the spinifex from Mount Liebig west to the Canning Stockroute, and south from a place called Sandy Blight Junction to Giles Weather Station, near the corner formed by the borders of South Australia, Western Australia and the Northern Territory. In that part of the world, any distance of less than a hundred miles is not counted. The men who worked on the track, the men who first frightened Gunia and Wadi with their mechanical dinosaur, have had their names perpetuated on a rough plaque, and I acknowledge my own gratitude by recording them here: Len Beadell (surveyor), Doug Stoneham (bulldozer), Scott Boord (grader), Rex Flatman (fitter), Frank Quinn (fuel supply), Paul Christensen (cook), Eric Graefling (driver), Lassie (The Dog). One also often heard the names of Bob Macaulay and W. V. ('Mac') McDougall, who patrolled the area from the Woomera rocket range.

The road construction company is financed by the Department of Supply, which is responsible for the rocket range. Its name, Gun Barrell, obviously comes from the fact that in places the track does not turn for many miles. Travel over much of it is still possible only in four-wheel-drive vehicles; nevertheless, the rough ridges have been ironed out, and I came to regard it almost as a highway when we returned to it on numerous occasions after 'scrub-bashing' through sandhills and huge-tufted spinifex. I was still more appreciative on realizing that Ted Evans, Jeremy Long, Dr John Hargrave and others had no such track to ease their passage during the 1957 expedition.

The Pintubi are constantly on the move. Because of the scarcity of food and water, one or the other is soon consumed in a given area, necessitating the movement of the entire group to new ground. This has resulted in a lack of development of any widespread use of spinifex or brush in the construction of dwellings. Generally, they build only windbreaks. In several hundred miles I saw only one crude 'room' built of spinifex and mulga around the base of a tree, which was used as the frame. This was at Kutitjara, about one hundred and eighty miles west of the Northern Territory border.

The equipment of the Pintubi consisted of hardwood spears, woomeras, throwing sticks (I did not see one boomerang), coolamons for carrying babies and pitchis for carrying water. There was no evidence of flint-tipped spears.

Their spiritual life is very much alive, although observance of it is made difficult and often impossible by the conditions of the desert. Deep reverence was apparent among men who showed us a sacred Dreaming, or totemic centre, known as Umari, and also as Old Man and His Wives Rocks.

The migratory habits of these people, and their numbers, can only be estimated. The survivors are thought not to exceed two hundred. Perhaps as many as two-thirds of those have already left the desert to live at Papunya, Yuendumu, Balgo Hills and Warburton, where they have established themselves in tribal communities, determined that their

language and culture will survive. Jeremy Long told me
that when isolated groups of Pintubi first arrived at Haasts
Bluff, before Papunya was built, their language dropped out
of use, but was revived to some extent when bigger parties
came in and reminded relatives of their own tongue.

Since coming into these centres the Pintubi have inter-
married with other groups and already the divisional lines
among the tribes, never clear-cut, have become thoroughly
blurred. The Pintubi complain that tribal neighbours are
always taking off their women. If that is so — and it has
certainly occurred several times and more often than the
reverse process — it is a condition to which they must
accustom themselves, like the men in subjugated civilized
lands during both hostile and friendly invasion.

Jeremy Long suggests that this phenomenon may be
basically a working out of demographic trends. The people
from the eastern fringes of the desert have suffered a
declining population in contact with white society, resulting
in tribes of high masculinity. The Pintubi have preserved in
their isolation a more normal balance of the sexes, and they
are now being used to redress the imbalance of the comparatively sophisticated groups.

He also says the congregation of multiple tribes on single
settlements has been possible only because the aborigines
have been able to abandon their precarious independence as
hunters and accept sedentary life on the fringes of white
society. The consequence of this change elsewhere in
Australia has normally been the almost total breakdown of
the ancient social structure, finely adjusted as it was to
nomadic hunting. The old men ruled because they were the
custodians of the practical and religious knowledge that
ensured survival in the desert. Inevitably, when food is
readily available from canteens and kitchens the old men

and their recondite knowledge of ritual and myth cease to hold their former status.

Aboriginal society in pre-European times was violent, and the influence of the old men was also based on their power to punish transgressors with death. Life at Papunya and Yuendumu is still occasionally turbulent and fights of varying intensity — with waddies, spears and cutting implements — are common. I was not surprised at a certain trepidation that Nosepeg felt when our vehicles for the return trip to Papunya were loaded with more than sixty spears. In spite of his avowal that they were strictly for the tourist trade he knew that their importation to the settlement would be frowned upon by the superintendent. Not that it stopped him; he set up his primitive arsenal in the desert every day and recruited fellow artisans to help him. The aborigines themselves admit that serious fights are now more frequent than in the times of wider dispersal. What they would be like without the restraints imposed by white man's law scarcely bears contemplation. I have seen men on these settlements — Wally and Jumbo Jabaljari are two of them — whose backs and shoulders have not one square inch of flesh that hasn't been scarred by vicious cuts.

In a monograph on the changing way of life of the people at Papunya, Jeremy Long writes that even the most lukewarm of the younger generation know that the elders will kill if necessary, and the fear of their claimed supernatural death-dealing powers is still very real.

He adds: 'Nevertheless, it is clear that there is much less conformity to the old laws and more defiance of the old men's authority than ever occurred in times before contact with white men. The first and most frequent challenge comes in the field of marriage choice. The aboriginal system of arranged marriages and preference of choice to mature men who held bargaining power was unnatural in the sense that it curbed free sexual selection, but was necessary in small and closely inter-related groups. Serious conflicts, sometimes persisting for months or years with periodical blood-letting, now result from a young man and woman defying the will of the elders and obstructing an arranged marriage.

'In the matter of contact with European civilization, the young more readily adjust to the demands of a new situation and earn prestige through performing new tasks. They thus have some weapons against the declining prestige and power of the old men when conflicts arise over women. Equally important in these conflicts between the generations are the attitudes of missions and government, as expressed by the white man on the spot or as understood by the aborigines.

'Frequently the older party to a dispute has one wife already. The younger can then assume that his stand will have the backing of the missionary and the mission-influenced aborigines, whose attitude is overtly against polygamy; furthermore, he is aware that, even though the authorities may be taking no action against polygamy, "one man — one wife" is the white man's custom. At the same time, both parties are aware that the normal resort to violence, with the risk of death for one of the parties, would be likely to lead to arrest and exile to another settlement, or imprisonment, for the other.

'In former times conflicts of this nature were probably rare though disputes between rival brothers — men with more or less equivalent rights — often occurred over women, and fatal spearings resulted. This was an accepted means of resolving such a conflict and the consequent reduction of the male population no doubt helped to make polygamy feasible.

'But where a young man defies the tribal custom now and disputes the issue with one who has all the force of tribal right on his side, he is relying on new elements in the social situation, induced by dependence in the final resort on the white man's law, to do something that was virtually unthinkable before. The effects of these changes in the balance of power are seen . . . in the higher proportion of men marrying in their late 'teens and early twenties, and in the appearance of widowers of some years standing — a rare phenomenon when the middle-aged dominated the marriage market.

'Initiation is the second major cause of conflict between the generations, and the guardians of tribal custom are here in a much stronger position. Only rarely does the dread of the threatened ordeals make a boy bold enough to defy opinion and evade the men who are responsible for apprehending him and supervising his initiation.

'As with white men, so the behaviour of aborigines is full of contradictions and paradoxes. Some of the customs of the white man are picked up apparently as easily as his clothes are put on and his food is eaten, but other beliefs and attitudes appear impervious to change. The economic and social changes that have been made as a result of contact have so far been in the nature of necessary adaptations to new situations. It has been a piecemeal process of initiation and acceptance.

'Whether the aborigines have the capacity for making wholesale revolutionary changes in their systems on beliefs and social organization by a conscious communal effort remains to be seen.'

These, then, were some of the problems already being faced by the Pintubi people who had left the desert in earlier years, and by their tribal neighbours. These were the conflicts that would have to be faced by any nomadic hunters with whom we hoped to make contact if they expressed a wish to be taken into the settlement.

I was grateful to Jeremy Long for such a lucid and

knowledgeable outline of the situation of the fringe dwellers. It was comforting to know that a man who had lived among and worked with Pintubi and Wailbri people for several years was leading our expedition. At least I would not be starved of well-based information and learned opinion about them. There was, however, one point on which I soon found myself in dispute with him, even though it was nothing more than a figure of speech. He had said that some of the customs of white men were picked up by the aborigines 'as easily as his clothes are put on'.

Within a few days I was to discover that a man who has been naked all his life does not readily — certainly not 'easily' — acquire the ability to put on clothes. In fact, they have as much idea of dressing themselves as a six months old baby.

Our First Contact

Four Land-Rovers were in our convoy which left Papunya on August 1, 1963, and began moving towards the sunset, but within forty-eight hours they were to be reduced to two. Our departure was delayed by mechanical trouble in one of them; two days later we were to lose it from a serious case of toothache in the transmission. The teeth of one of the gears began falling out and were ground into small pieces by the others. Eventually the vehicle had to be towed back to base.

A fourth Land-Rover was with us for only part of the distance to establish a fuel and water dump at Sandy Blight Junction. This was driven by John Pender, manager of the Haasts Bluff cattle station run by the Welfare Branch, and John Chambers, the head stockman. On the night before our departure we spent an exceedingly pleasant interlude as guests of John and Doreen Pender in the old Haasts Bluff homestead, in the midst of what is perhaps the most breath-takingly beautiful scenery in the Northern Territory — the heart of the Namatjira country. That was also my last sleep in a bed for almost a fortnight; thereafter we camped beside the track, rolling out our swags in the red dust and building big fires of mulga and desert oak. John and Doreen Pender welcomed us warmly, although there were two babies in the house. I have a feeling that that night I was guilty of a considerable flow of words. I remember telling stories until a late hour, encouraged by John's spontaneous laughter.

If I offended, however, I paid the price two nights later when John himself took over the story-telling in our camp at a place called Wiyanbiri. Never, in more than twenty years in the Australian bush, have I listened to such a torrent of uninhibited men-only yarns, told with explosive and vivid gusto.

Our party consisted of Jeremy Long, B.A., leader; Gordon Grimwade, a cadet patrol officer; Frank Few, an American cine-cameraman employed by the Australian Broadcasting Commission; Douglas Lockwood, reporter and cook; John Pender and John Chambers on the supply vehicle; Junkata (Nosepeg) Juburula, interpreter of tracks, smokes and language, and philosopher-extraordinary; Snowy Jambajimba, driver; Tim Karmin-nalba, interpreter; Nawi Juburula, guide; Ngugudi (One-Arm) Juburula, guide; and Jalyuri Jabaljari, guide. Tim, Nawi and Ngugudi returned to Papunya with Pender and Chambers when our third vehicle broke down. Snowy did his best to further reduce our mobility by driving one of the trucks along a sandy track with the handbrake on. I made him stop when smoke began pouring past the petrol tanks and through the cabin. We had sixty gallons of petrol and thousands of feet of cine film on board. In these circumstances, if there was to be a fire, I thought it wise not to be in the truck. Frank Few would not have been pleased to lose his film, especially as hundreds of feet had already been exposed and couldn't be repeated. Furthermore, Ruth Lockwood may not have been pleased to lose her husband. So we waited until the boiling oil subsided and the red-hot parts cooled off.

Soon after lunch on our first day the magnificent blue peaks of Mt Liebig, known to the natives as Amundurrnga, were towering above us. It was here that we saw our last permanent water, in a bore used for watering stock. Not until we reached Jupiter Well, about four hundred miles away across the desert, would we see more than a few gallons, none of it permanent, in rockholes and soaks. We carried fifteen gallons in each vehicle and dumped eighty gallons at Sandy Blight junction.

Late in the afternoon we saw kangaroos; and Jeremy Long wounded one with a ·22 rifle. Nosepeg ran after it but it got away. He came back and spat with disgust. 'Boomerang more better!' he said. I knew he didn't believe that, especially when, a short time later, Long killed a big one for that night's dinner.

At our camp at Wiyanbiri the kangaroo was cooked over a blazing fire, fur and all. Nawi took the tail, with its charred fur, and began tearing at it with his teeth. Nosepeg, tired from the hunt, was already asleep. Tim cut the carcass with knives struck by hammers, and then asked, 'Who got this kangaroo?'

'Nosepeg,' I said, and realized at once that I had made a mistake. 'Jerry Long shot it,' I added. 'Nosepeg carried it back to the truck.'

Tim was not reassured. He threw down the knives and stopped work. As far as he was concerned, the kangaroo belonged to Nosepeg and he alone could divide it.

Nosepeg, lying on his blanket by the fire, must have overheard. He spoke in the dialect — permission, obviously, for Tim to proceed. Soon the great half-cooked haunches and ribs were being passed around, but I was impressed, nevertheless, by this intrusion of the ancient tribal law under which various portions of an animal were allotted to predetermined owners, with the successful hunter traditionally entitled to first choice.

Killing a kangaroo on the first day out was a big help in our make-believe pantry, especially as next day's break down of one of the vehicles meant jettisoning a considerable quantity of tinned food. The gamey fresh meat was also a comfort to the aborigines, who carried pieces of it for several days, constantly gnawing at great hunks of beef so under-done as to be almost alive. Later, when we shot other kanga-roos, it occurred to me that the degree to which an aboriginal cooked his food could depend largely on his appetite. Very hungry men like kangaroo steak underdone for the simple reason that they cannot long delay eating after the fur has been charred and their nostrils are assailed by the first aroma of grilling flesh. A man who has recently eaten is more likely to have his food well done.

If the aborigines had the physical comfort of good food and a warm fire, we had ours, too. Frank Few startled us all by turning on electric light (a luxury we were to share every night of the trip) and dry Martinis! One of the biggest items of his incredible equipment was a petrol-driven generator to charge the batteries which drove his camera. While the batteries were being charged the generator doubled as an electric light plant. Each of us had a personal light, and on several occasions the natives' camp was also illuminated. I'll never forget the incredulous surprise on the faces of desert people who had not seen night-light brighter than their campfire when Frank switched on what he fondly called his S.E.C. (State Electricity Commission). The Mar-tinis, as dry as the desert, were served in crystal goblets and complete with an olive on a toothpick. I trumped him with a bottle of bushman's rum, but stayed awake to regret it; John Pender, already in full verbal flight, might have been drinking words instead of rum, for they bubbled from him late into the night like champagne from a magnum.

Also in Few's equipment, which overflowed from his truck and into ours, were two small walkie-talkie transceivers. Their range was limited, but they were handy in communi-cating between moving vehicles. And they fascinated the aborigines beyond belief. Nosepeg was beside himself with

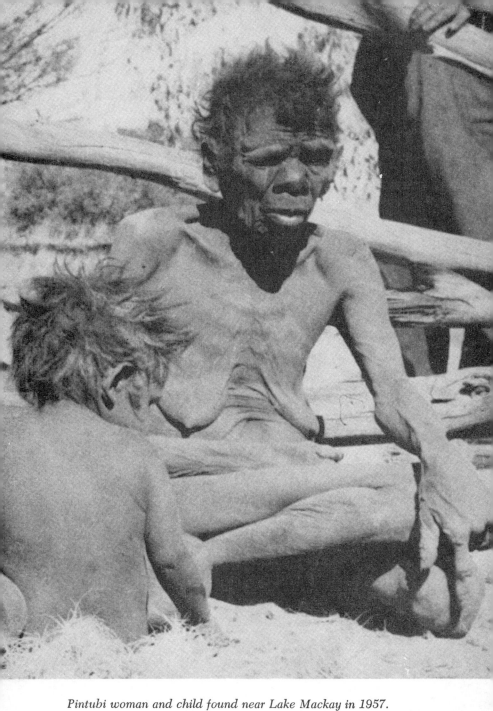

Pintubi woman and child found near Lake Mackay in 1957.

(E. C. Evans *photo.*)

Man at Papunya. He had been out of the desert only a few weeks, and spoke in whispers.

. . . but not these. They have been at Yuendumu since 1957 and have lost their shyness.

joy when I talked to him through one of these sets and he heard his own name. Then he pressed the 'sending' button and exclaimed, 'Goodness. Proper! Proper!'

For reasons I could readily understand, the natives were less impressed with the greater magic of a polaroid camera carried by Jeremy Long. To desert people who had never seen photographs of any kind it meant little. How could men who had no knowledge of the chemical processes necessary in the production of conventional photographs be impressed by snapshots of themselves which came almost instantly from the back of the camera which took them? They displayed scant interest when Long showed them their own portraits within seconds of pressing the shutter; their attitude was clearly, 'Show us something clever, like a tin of food.' Frank Few did show them something clever: a returning boomerang which he threw with considerable skill and caught on the rebound. This was magic they understood; they killed game with throwing sticks and killing boomerangs, but I doubt if any of them had ever seen the returning type used by sophisticated aborigines elsewhere.

We woke on that first morning of the long desert journey in a grove of dense mulga. We were only a hundred miles from Papunya and two hundred and fifty miles from Alice Springs, yet beside my swag I found embedded in the ground a flat stone deeply grooved by constant grinding.

'The people use that for grinding berries and other bush tucker,' Nosepeg explained.

In the same area we found the remains of a stone axe. We were still close to civilization, and yet, I thought, we had already penetrated The Place of Primitive Men. Just to prove me wrong, our portable transceiver was switched on. The Royal Flying Doctor Base at Alice Springs was calling for 'medicals', and then for normal telegraphic traffic from

stations as remote as ours. Parts were being ordered for
motor vehicles. Someone five hundred miles from us was
receiving birthday greetings. A station owner was telling his
manager to expect him that day. Jeremy Long spoke to his
wife, Frances, at Haasts Bluff. But within a few hours we
were signalling with less complex equipment: Smoke. It was
the only kind of signal likely to be received and understood
by the people with whom we wished to make contact.

Near a place called Ilbili, unmarked on our map, Nosepeg
surveyed what might have been the eastern boundary of
Pintubi tribal country, once his own, and asked Long to stop
the vehicle. Then he demanded matches, shouted something
about 'Proper good waru!' (fire or smoke) and soon had an
acre of spinifex blazing and billowing black smoke. I was to
learn that you don't just light a fire anywhere and expect
good signals; you must choose the right density of spinifex
at the right stage of dryness. This was our first attempt at
communicating with people we couldn't see by the method
of the Stone Age. We thought it improbable that the nearest
Pintubi family was within a hundred miles, and our signal
would therefore not be seen. However, there was a chance
that groups on walkabout east of the country in which we
expected to find them might see our message and converge
on our track. This first smoke caused much excitement
among the Pintubi with us. They had listened that morning
to the wireless messages flashing to and from Alice Springs;
now they were using their own means to talk to tribesmen.
It should be clearly understood, however, that these smoke
signals do not say anything beyond advertising a man's
presence in an approximate locality; smoke is so erratically
affected by wind, time and distance that the old idea of
sending decipherable messages is strictly for the cartoonists.

The resinous, highly aromatic spinifex, burning furiously,
pervaded the nostrils. In a land where sounds and scents

were amplified and intensified because of the stillness and the clear air, the smell of spinifex was overwhelming. Nearby, we found the first signs of aboriginal food in its natural state — black seeds of the Bangkuna bush which had been baked in ashes and ground on a hollowed stone. Nosepeg picked some up and ate them. 'Number one bush tucker,' he said.

In this country, the aboriginal mind is entirely preoccupied with food and water (kapi). Localities, almost invariably, are known by their waterholes. Seldom does a place have a name at all unless water is present or has been present.

Driving along our track we came to the Wilbia locality, named for a rockhole, which was roughly ten miles to the south in dense scrub. Nosepeg took us there, without any noticeable features to guide him, with an unerring sense of direction. As we drove through the mulga he gave instructions to Jeremy Long with his finger, with both hands if he wanted us to go straight ahead, and sometimes by pointing with his mouth. He identified kangaroo, emu and goanna tracks, and became quite excited when he saw numerous fresh dingo tracks.

'Lot of puppies! Lot of puppies! Let's get them!' he said.

'We've got plenty of tucker on the truck,' I said, assuming incorrectly that he wanted them to eat.

'No more! One pound for each scalp. Mobs of money!" he said.

Nosepeg is a sophisticated man. He is also an astute trader. He knows the value of money, and understands the government bounty for dingo scalps.

After an hour of travelling I thought Nosepeg must have lost his way, but he did not hesitate in giving directions. Eventually we broke through to a spinifex plain, from which there rose a low rock formation.

'Wilbia,' he said. 'Plenty of water in that rockhole.'

But this was one of Nosepeg's infrequent errors, for the hole was dry. We dug into the cool damp soil but did not reach water. I wondered how aborigines felt about it when that happened to them after walking fifty miles from the last water, knowing that the next, which could also be dry, was twenty miles further on. Little wonder that they perished — and are still perishing — while moving from one locality to another after the food supply in one has been depleted.

Two hours later and perhaps thirty miles from where we lit it, we could still see our big black smoke. It had risen hundreds of feet in the air and spread laterally in the cooler layers, an astro-beacon as prominent as the brightest neon, a sign which must be seen by aborigines if there were any in the area. And then, obligingly, it was answered.

We had been driving for only ten minutes after a break for lunch when Jalyuri, one of the Pintubi guides, banged heavily on the roof of our vehicle. We thought a swag may have fallen off, and stopped to investigate.

'Waru! Waru!' he shouted. 'Smoke! Smoke!'

Since our dense black smoke billowed up Jalyuri, sitting on the back of the truck, had been watching the horizon constantly; now he was first to see what we all hoped to find.

By straining my eyes, I could see a faint wisp of smoke, perhaps twenty, perhaps fifty miles away to the north. It meant nothing to me. If alone, I would have dismissed it as a bushfire. But to these hawk-eyed aborigines bushfires don't happen. They are caused — and generally by other human beings.

Nosepeg pointed towards it. 'There are people at that spot. I don't know who they are, but there must be people,' he said. 'They have seen our smoke and are letting us know they're there."

Our own signal now hung heavily black on the horizon.

Our track bisected the oceans of spinifex like a great red wake, seldom deviating, a plumb-bob leading us straight towards these Stone Age people who had been in the desert since the Time of Dream — for thousands of years before white men came to Australia. I had seen their relatives, the primitives who had walked and pole-vaulted into Papunya and Yuendumu several years earlier, there to learn for the first time that in the twentieth century of the white man's calendar there had been two world wars fought with weapons they had never seen or heard of, that the country they lived in was named Australia, and that there were many other tribes of black people as well as white people in nations which could only be reached by crossing oceans they could not comprehend.

Now that smoke in the north-west sky held the promise that I might soon meet other people who had still not heard of these things; people who perhaps had not seen a white skin or a motor vehicle. I was overcome with excitement at the prospect. It is not every man's privilege, more than half way through the century, to greet men for whom you represent a new species.

Having seen the smoke, it was evident that the guides with us ignored it to concentrate on another search: for tracks of the people who had caused it. Nosepeg had been sitting between Jeremy Long and me in the cabin of the truck, but he transferred to the back with Jalyuri to get a better view of the soft red earth around us — the earth which, they now expected, would soon bear the imprint of human feet.

A few minutes later the roof resounded again and Nosepeg shouted. 'Man tracks! Man tracks!'

We stopped. Nosepeg climbed down, but Jalyuri remained on his perch. Nosepeg briefly examined the tracks in the sand. They had been made by a bare human foot, and appeared to be recent. The natives had obviously taken that much in with their first glance; the more detailed examination was necessary for quite another purpose. Nosepeg soon let us know what that was. Incredibly, he named the man who made them.

'It's the Jagamara man,' he said. 'He has two wives. He is the son of Gurabi of the Juburula skin who lives at Yuendumu.'

'Impossible!' I said.

'I tell you it's the Jagamara man,' he repeated. I could see that he was a little hurt that I should question his identification of one whose tracks he had clearly seen. When I pressed him he gave me the man's personal name as well as his skin name.

'Jugudi,' Nosepeg said. 'Jagamara man.'

The fact that Nosepeg could identify the stranger by his personal name was proof that he knew him, for personal names are seldom used in the tribes. Jalyuri's name, for instance, was really that of his dog; he would not be so immodest as to use his own, even though he had several, one of which would be secret and known only to tribal elders. In subsequent questioning of the Pintubi I was given other names which belonged to dogs.

The leading Australian anthropologist, Professor A. P. Elkin, says that there is a general disinclination by the aborigines to the use of the personal name. On one occasion he recorded a whole genealogy with the correct references to the spirit-home, local country, moiety and totems of more than twenty individuals, and with what purported to be their personal names, only to realize later that in every case he had been given a nickname. Professor Elkin believes the objection to use of the personal name belongs mainly to the realm of the secret life, for names are usually taken from sacred mythological and totemic associations, and therefore must not be bandied about. He says they represent the real self which belongs to the spiritual and sacred sphere, not to the world of everyday affairs. For the latter, kinship terms, subsection (what I have called 'skin') names, or nicknames suffice. Professor Elkin says that in some areas there is a fear lest magical use could be made of the personal name to hurt its owner; it is therefore never mentioned except in a whisper and then only in the presence of men of the same group.

I think my scepticism about Nosepeg's ability to identify a man by his footprints was understandable in one who had not observed these experts working. After all, Nosepeg lived at Papunya and, I presumed, did not often visit this country. In any case, it seemed beyond belief that a man could look at another's tracks and identify him positively. My education in these matters began that day. I was to learn that when an aboriginal said tracks belonged to a certain man there was little likelihood that he would be mistaken. Three hundred miles further west Nosepeg and Jalyuri correctly named the owners of other tracks we saw.

They also demonstrated that they possessed better than average powers of reasoning. If I wished to talk to a man who had advertised his position with smoke I would go towards it. Nosepeg suggested we try the opposite direction, for that way lay the only waterhole in the vicinity. The Jaga-mara would eventually return there, and his family would probably be already in residence. So that is where we went — to Wili rockhole, renamed Kumanadja because a man named Wili had died there recently. That name was no longer used because it reminded the living of the dead, and of their grief. We were careful, so as not to offend the aboriginal sensibilities, to call it Kumanadja, too.

The Kintore Ranges were rising blue against the south-west sky, only a few miles from the Western Australian

border. Mulga, stunted desert oaks and corkwoods grew
sparsely, but there was no sign of any other living thing. Yet
here we found the tracks of a human being who supported
himself and a family by his wits and hunting cunning in
this harshest of Australian deserts.

Kumanadja rockhole was five miles south of our track. We
bumped over spinifex and the tangerine ground and soon
picked up a series of footprints. Then Jalyuri and Nosepeg
banged on the roof together.

"Piccaninny there!"

I looked where they pointed and one hundred yards away
saw what appeared to be a burnt stump. But it moved, and
I knew it to be human, a naked child. A small woman
appeared from the shadows carrying another child, walking
briskly through the spinifex on a course which would
converge with ours near the rockhole.

Here was a woman of the desert with two children. I was
anxious to go to her as soon as the truck stopped and begin
my impatient questioning. Jeremy Long, practised in such
matters, sat down instead and appeared to be taking little
notice. This was one of my first lessons in the observance of
conventions when meeting strange aborigines in the bush.
Long knew that Jalyuri was the woman's brother. He must
therefore be first to greet her.

Fifty yards from the rockhole, which we had reached, the
woman sat down with the children and turned her back to
us. Jalyuri walked slowly towards her and approached to
within five yards. He also sat down, with his back to the
woman, facing us. As far as I could see, he did not greet her
except by finger-talk. After a few minutes they began
conversing.

When I approached she showed no shyness and welcomed
me with a pleasant smile which I realized at once came from
a woman still living in the Stone Age. We were then only

three hundred miles west of Alice Springs, but civilization
had not yet penetrated to that point.

The woman was wearing a tattered dress given to her by
relatives. The children were naked. The family and their
families before them had hunted in this desert for generations. It was theirs. They knew it, and understood it, and
were aware that it would kill them unless they were always
careful — and lucky.

Like Gunia and Wadi, this family had hidden under spinifex bushes when frightened by aeroplanes. They, too, had
seen the road grader and scampered for the remoter sandhills.

Kumanadja rockhole was not more than three feet in
diameter and about five feet deep. It would be dry before
the first of the summer rains — if they came at all. For that
reason, the surrounding country could not support more than
one family. When the water dried they would be forced to
move elsewhere, west to Pinpirrnga or east to Wilbia — and
when they got there, as we discovered, the last drops may
have disappeared in the sand. Frantically, then, they would
try to reach the next water, fearful that it, too, would be dry.

What an existence, to be precariously placed in a treacherous desert where the threat of perishing was constantly
present! For a man to live in these circumstances was difficult enough, but for women and children to do so was
nothing short of an incredible feat of survival. Babies were
born here and grew to maturity as men and women, learning
and sharing their rituals when the seasons permitted, fighting
always for life against thirst and slow starvation. The single
primary lesson taught in all their schools was aimed at
implanting the will to live and the ability to survive.

Half an hour later we saw another stately figure moving
towards us through the bush. She was the Jagamara's second
wife, who had been hunting, apparently without success.

This was unusual because, while the men are magnificent hunters, the women in most tribes are recognized as being even better. In many areas before detribalization they supplied the basic foods like lily roots, yams, berries, reptiles and small animals while the men concentrated on bigger game. This was equally true of the women of the desert. One was recently known to have returned from a day's hunt with fifteen goannas. Her husband had three.

With the arrival of his second wife, the Jagamara's entire family was present, but he still hunted. The woman went directly to their 'camp', a crude windbreak of mulga and spinifex not more than two feet high, three 'beds' scooped from the sand close together, and four fires to the three beds — one on each side of the man and his two wives.

The equipment of this primitive 'house' consisted of a grinding stone, a coolamon, a tin dish acquired from somewhere and filled with water, and a dozen spears. Nothing else.

A little later the two wives came to sit near Nosepeg's and Jalyuri's camp — but not too close.

By the standards of the aboriginal women from the 'big-water, plenty-tucker' places of the north like Melville, Bathurst and Groote Islands and especially the Anula at Borroloola, they were unattractive. But they were actually pretty when I was able, later, to compare their appearance with the other Pintubi women we met in the desert, most of whom were ugly.

The first wife, Pararanga, was less than five feet tall, but she was nursing a child and had big pendulous breasts. She smiled pleasantly and almost constantly. This was also in direct contrast to the other Pintubi women, whose doleful aspect depressed me. The second wife, Murmuya, was the elder and taller of the two and of heavier build. She also smiled pleasantly, and took a keen interest in everything that happened. Both had the straight hair typical of the Central Australian people. They had fine white teeth which had never been brushed.

Nosepeg, the soft-hearted old sophisticate, was already making a damper. Snowy, Nawi, Jalyuri, Tim and Ngugudi watched him.

'I'm supposed to be the boss of this lot, but they let me do all the work,' Nosepeg complained. I was to be with him long enough to discover that, in fact, idleness was foreign to him.

When the damper was ready the women and children were given huge chunks of it, and thus began a meal of white man's food. They had already been given a haunch of kangaroo, which the Number One wife carried on her head. The damper was spread with a mixture of kangaroo meat, jam and condensed milk — and they thought it was Christmas. The women ate slowly, and for a long time.

We thought that the Jagamara, after an unsuccessful hunt, might sleep on the ground many miles from his family who, if we had not arrived, would have spent a hungry night — and I'm sure it would not have been their first. However, we knew he had seen our smoke and we expected he would try to get back, even if that meant walking — or running — twenty miles.

The earth had taken its first big bite from the setting sun when I saw a black figure striding magnificently across the skyline. He walked, but his pace suggested a trot.

'The Jagamara!' Nosepeg said. 'He comes.'

Jalyuri, his brother-in-law, had already seen him but said nothing. Except for Nosepeg, who is garrulous, the Pintubi are not naturally talkative people.

The Jagamara went directly to his own camp, fifty yards from ours. He threw his spears into the windbreak and flopped onto his bed for this night and every other night of

his life — the ground. But I could see that he first unhitched
the result of the day's hunt from his waist and threw it down:
a rabbit and five small goannas. His family, after all, would
already have eaten. What is more, they would have had the
comparatively rare delicacy of a rabbit. We saw a number
of warrens during the trip, but in the twelve hundred miles
I travelled from leaving Alice Springs until returning there,
I did not see another rabbit. This man had caught one. But at
what tremendous expenditure of effort! Jugudi and his
family (I have no qualms about using his personal name) had
arrived at Kumanadja rockhole only the night before after
walking thirty miles from Pinpirrnga. Fortunately, the rocks
still held a little water. The tired children, the tireless wives
and the alert hunter could drink, although a man and a
young girl had only recently perished in the same area.

Next morning — the day of our arrival — was like any
other in this nomad's life. The family could not eat until he
or his wives had tracked and killed game. He must have left
at dawn, carrying only his spears. He returned at dusk with
the rabbit and five goannas. We knew by the distance to his
smoke that he had walked about forty miles. His chest
heaved; he seemed near to exhaustion.

He was about five feet nine inches tall — the tallest of all
the men we saw. His body, while not obviously malnourished, did not carry one ounce of superfluous flesh. His
fine thighs tapered to slender calves and ankles. In view of
his long daily walks for food, I expected that both would
have been more heavily muscular. He resembled Jalyuri in
appearance and, to a lesser extent, the 'soft-faced' man,
Gunia, I had met at Papunya. He smiled readily and posed
for photographs, but I think he was looking forward to a
long rest.

The day before they had eaten a dingo and its litter of

pups. A few days earlier there had been a Feral cat on the menu.

A dish containing half a gallon of water was in Jugudi's camp when I inspected it. Now when I returned there to greet him it was empty, but his thirst wasn't yet quenched because he also drank a billyful we supplied.

One could not do other than admire the independent spirit of this bearded, magnificent man, his matted hair tied with grass string. He earned his family's bread as the Neanderthals had millennia ago with Stone Age weapons. He asked no favours of anyone.

As Jeremy Long said, 'It's a long time since he called anyone Boss.'

I was aware, also, of a profound respect for his intelligence. For I knew that he would survive in the desert long after all white men and most detribalized aborigines had perished. Yet he was completely modest, unaware that he had done anything remarkable by finding food for a family where apparently none existed.

After supper he led his small son to Nosepeg's camp. His wives and daughter, unequal in all tribal life, remained in theirs. Jugudi spent a carefree evening with his brother-in-law, Jalyuri, and the other aborigines with us, knowing that tomorrow he could have a rare day of rest from the eternal hunt. There would be damper and tea and a haunch of kangaroo which had fallen to a white man's bullet by a method he did not understand.

There were two other striking pieces of evidence to confirm the utter primitiveness of these people.

I gave Jugudi a cigarette and held a lighted match for him. But he did not know that to light a cigarette it helps if you puff.

Jalyuri gave the small boy, his nephew, an old shirt many

sizes too big for him. I watched while the naked lad tried to put it on, and was fascinated by one of the most extraordinary exhibitions I have seen. He had no idea what to do. At first he put it on his head and then tried to fight his way out. Next he got his head into an armhole, but could get it no farther. Told to use his arms, he wrapped the shirt around one like an ungainly bandage. That didn't look right, either, so he took it off again. Only with the help of two men did he eventually get both arms into the sleeves. I'm not sure that I fully succeeded in suppressing my rude laughter, for this boy, at the age of six, was struggling manfully to wear the first garment he had owned in his life.

His father was dressed in strips of an old singlet and a grass string supporting a brief pubic cloth. The string had utility value as an aid to carrying game — the rabbit and goannas were hanging from it — but the rest of his clothes were worn for decoration only. Frankly, he would have been a better looking man without them.

Around his head he wore a band of corded grass to keep his hair in place. If I'd had a hat I would gladly have given it to him, if only to show that I regarded him as the kind of man worthy of the C. J. Dennis tribute: 'I dips me lid.'

Jugudi Chooses Civilization

Jugudi was welcome to my hat, but I'd have given the rest of my wardrobe in exchange for the ability to understand the conversation in the natives' camp that night. Normally they were asleep before us, stretching out on their blankets, close to the warming fires, with bellies full of kangaroo, damper and white man's tinned 'tucker'. An aboriginal who is warm and has eaten well is soon overcome by sleep. They often slept in the sun after lunch, and Nosepeg occasionally had a cat-nap in the truck as we bumped along. But that night the talk seemed endless. I have no doubt that Jugudi told detailed stories about his life in the desert, perhaps of how he had survived with his family in the times of Big Drought, although drought is normal in their lives. He had recently been through one of several years' duration, with average falls of not more than two or three inches a year. How had they managed for water when the rockholes and the soaks had dried up? Were they affected by the intensely hot summers in a country which offered little shade? How was it possible for a man to hunt in almost waterless country when sun temperatures were constantly above one hundred and fifty degrees? Oh, for a knowledge of the Pintubi language, to have learnt these things first-hand from Jugudi, and to have been able to follow his reactions as he was told by the others of the marvels and magic of civilization. Instead, I had to be satisfied with Nosepeg's interpretations.

Towards midnight Jugudi went 'home' to his wives; that is, he moved from one camp on the ground to another. The talk stopped and I could hope to sleep — but not for long. The night was cold and the fires were stoked about 4 a.m. I was warm in my sleeping bag, but a strong south-east wind was blowing and I wondered if Jugudi and his family were cold. The children would sleep with their mothers, between fires built almost on top of them, but they had no blankets and only one flimsy garment each. The ground seemed less hard to me after that; whatever my discomforts, they were nothing compared with theirs. It must have been a miserable night for them, yet they had not known any other way of life. At that time, of course, I had no idea that Jugudi's living conditions would appear reasonably civilized by the standards of other families of nomads we were to find in the heart of the Gibson Desert.

The dawn scene must have been a strange one to Jugudi and his wives, Murmuya and Pararanga. They could normally expect to see nothing outside their campfire circle but the endless spinifex and stunted bush. Now there were four motor vehicles and white men rugged in several layers of warm clothes; a wireless was soon to begin its inexplicable crackling and the voice of an unseen man would be heard through the camp area; tins would be opened and found to contain goanna already stewed — well, if not goanna, then the white man's equivalent of it. A movie camera whirred and still cameras clicked, and I wouldn't be surprised if Jugudi thought they were machines which made the tinned food. How could the children know that the white dust they saw converted by Nosepeg into a damper fit for kings was made of flour which came from wheat grown on blacksoil plains in the Victorian Wimmera? They had never seen flour or wheat, and in the red and tangerine desert there is no black soil. I wondered if they knew that soil colours did change to black, for out here there was none.

Jugudi had acquired a shirt and trousers — not new, to be sure, and certainly not clean, but at least whole. I was glad to see that his tattered singlet and loin cloth had fallen off; I preferred him naturally naked to the caricature he became in what he thought passed for garments.

Murmuya had been naked yesterday except for a pubic cloth. Miraculously, she now wore not one dress but two. These clothes had apparently been in the swags of our aboriginal guides. They were given to the desert people not to start them on the road towards modesty, but simply to keep them warm. In the next week or so I was to regard the swags as having false bottoms, for clothes continued to be produced from them when it seemed obvious that they contained only blankets.

Jugudi's rabbit and goannas were eaten for breakfast, the rabbit lightly grilled, fur and all, on an open fire, and the goannas baked in hot ashes. But that's not all they had for breakfast. An enormous quantity of damper and baked kangaroo also disappeared. (The kangaroo was one we had shot two days earlier. Jugudi said they were rare in his hunting domain.)

Was it the taste of this damper that persuaded Jugudi to leave the desert? Exotic food, after all, has made white men do stranger things. It is well known to have affected the course of history. Jugudi might have decided that he could not live without damper, this magnificent concoction of flour and water and baking powder. Whatever the reason, he let Jeremy Long know that he would like to take his family into the settlement at Papunya where, for all he knew, flour might grow on trees. He was tired of hunting in the desert. His youngest child had been badly burnt on the back of the hand; she had put it in the coals of the campfire while asleep and, like other aborigines we were to meet, was horribly scarred. There are no salves or medicines in that country. At Papunya the two children, their mothers and father would have adequate medical attention. It was possible, though unlikely, that Jugudi's wives would give birth to future children in the aseptic whiteness of the settlement hospital instead of on a couch of bark and leaves in the bush, one of them caring for the other in her hour of travail, pounding on an abdomen which would henceforth be distended only in pregnancy, and not by malnutrition, until a child was born — a child whose only shawl would be of red sand, a child who would begin a lifelong fight for survival against intense cold or insufferable heat on its very first day in the world. It was possible, I said, though not likely, that Jugudi's wives would accept the hospital for their next confinements. They were desert nomads who would be frightened of the enclosing walls and the inexplicable gadgetry of a maternity ward. But the man's daughters and grand-daughters, having first been through the settlement school, having accustomed themselves to the once-strange ways, will almost certainly welcome the comfort of a bed and the reassurance of a trained nurse when the magical seed in their bodies is ready to be emitted in human form.

And so, before we left, Jugudi put his wives and children on John Pender's vehicle which was to return east that day and began what was, for them, the biggest adventure of their lives. The children cried miserably with fear — the kind of fear a white child might know on its first aeroplane flight — for this was their first ride in a motor vehicle. I did not blame them for being afraid of a catastrophe. Jugudi strapped his spears to the side of the truck and climbed aboard, too. Although he wore clothes, without those weapons he might have seemed naked. They were as much a part of him as his long beard, his knotted hair bound with grass braid, and eyes and hands practised in the arts of tracking and killing.

I was glad their future lives were to be less harsh. I was glad that at Papunya they would no longer be often close to starvation, and intolerably thirsty in summer heat because they could not carry enough water while hunting. They would still hunt — the women, too — for this was inherent in them. But when they failed to catch game there would be other food available, and while walking they could carry water in man-made billies fitted with handles and lids and filled from man-made taps which gushed miraculously when turned.

Yet I was also sad that these people were leaving, for the desert was losing men and women of stature. I felt it would be a poorer place; that the desert would miss this self-reliant soft-faced man who had overcome its dangers by learning its secrets.

There would now be one family less who had never seen a white man's house or a sedan motor car or a white woman or fences or tarred roads or electric light. They would learn that an aeroplane is not a flying animal but an aerial bus. One would land regularly at Papunya settlement. After their initial fright, and on being reassured by relatives, they would go to see it, to stand close to the horrifying thing that had sent them scuttling in terror under the spinifex when they first saw it flying across their land. Tractors and road-graders would become commonplace; they would learn the value of money and how to spend it in the canteen; the children would learn in a foreign language called English that it was possible to count beyond three, and to express abstract thoughts.

And yet, as I say, I was sad. For these people would also quickly acquire some of the addictions and bad habits of civilized society after tasting its opiates. They could be preyed upon by unscrupulous people of their own race, and become involved in fights provoked by disparities in the disposal of tribal women, although these were not unknown in the desert. Finally, their children and grand-children, in acquiring the skills necessary to their subsistence in the new world, would assuredly lose those that had keep their fore-fathers alive in the desert for generations — the primary skill of hunting which had made possible the survival of the tribes since the Time of Dream.

We left Kumanadja rockhole that morning with four vehicles. We expected to be reduced to three on returning to the Gun Barrell Road, where John Pender and John Chambers would turn east while we turned west. But it was at that point that our third vehicle developed the toothache I have already mentioned, making necessary a quick change in our loading of people, petrol, and pork and beans. Fortu-nately Pender and Chambers were still with us and were able to take Nawi, Ngugudi and Tim back to Papunya. The breakdown was a blow to our provisioning — and therefore our endurance — especially as our Number Two vehicle was also suspect. In any respectable fleet it would have been changed from second to second last. My only criticism of the arrangements for the entire trip is the lack of consideration for Long and his party by the transport authorities. This was a patrol to the remotest heart of the continent, yet two of the vehicles allotted to us should not have been sent off main roads. One had to be patched up before we left Papunya, and in the desert overheated so badly that the engine continued running for seconds after the ignition was switched off. The other had to be abandoned, and towed back. Instead of being given the best vehicles available for a journey which would obviously be rough, and perhaps even dangerous, Long had to be satisfied with only one in good order, and two that were questionable and, as events proved, thoroughly unsatisfactory for the tracks ahead of us. It was typical of the state of our Number Two that Frank Few and Jeremy Long often had their heads and hands inside the engine. We towed it to start the motor, and used sticky-tape to secure the main lead to the coil.

In these circumstances, I was pleased that Jalyuri remained with us to go on into Western Australia. If we were to have further breakdowns and eventually exhaust our food supply, it would be reassuring to have a professional hunter with us — a man who, in the past year, had been living like Jugudi as a nomad. He knew the desert. He knew where to find water and goannas and dingoes. Grilled goanna and baked dingo might not taste like the chicken served in government hostels in Alice Springs, but both will keep you alive for a long time.

In spite of these troubles, our progress along the Gun Barrell road was good. We averaged about twenty miles an hour, and sometimes reached forty. The track is so seldom used that we dumped a hundred and twenty gallons of fuel and eighty gallons of water beside it and felt confident it would still be there when we returned a fortnight later. It was.

This dump was established at a place aptly called Sandy Blight Junction. As far as one could see there was red sand, red soil and spinifex. I wouldn't be surprised to learn that the Gun Barrell man who named it, probably Len Beadell, was stricken with sandy blight at that point. A sign post told us we were at S. 23 degrees 11 minutes 58 seconds and E. 129 degrees 33 minutes 35 seconds. I thanked Beadell for pin-pointing our position so clearly, for without it I knew only that I was far from home. The Kintore Ranges were close by and the Western Australian border only thirty-six miles ahead.

From Sandy Blight, a graded track led south for 252 miles to Giles weather station, with nothing in between. It was 350 miles west to the Canning stockroute, which we almost reached, and more than three hundred miles east to Alice Springs. Whichever direction you travelled, it was wise to be equipped with four efficient wheels rather than two boots.

As we refuelled, Nosepeg and Jalyuri walked a short distance down the road to Giles, much as more sophisticated passengers in less remote places might walk to the corner pub or through the Botanical Gardens while their bus is being serviced. That was quite out of character for Jalyuri, an expert at conserving his energy. When we stopped beside our western track Jalyuri was generally last to climb down from his seat on the back of the truck. When he did descend he could be guaranteed to be lying in the sand within a few moments, doing his best, and usually succeeding, to go to sleep in the sun. If the day was cold, he built a small fire and curled up around it. To see him taking exercise with Nosepeg was therefore something of a novelty.

When they returned Nosepeg apprenticed me as Assistant Smoke-Maker. He handed me my own box of matches and told me to start making smoke in the spinifex. I threw matches wildly into the long porcupine grass, but Nosepeg either wasn't satisfied with the result or wanted to demonstrate his authority over a white man in front of the other aborigines. He grumbled that I was a useless whitefeller, picked up a blazing torch of dried leaves, and began spreading destruction over the countryside.

'Good smoke now,' he said. 'Blackfeller will understand my talk. He couldn't understand that whitefeller rubbish.'

Shortly after noon we crossed from the Northern Territory

into Western Australia. Two years ago the border was unmarked. Today there is a sign erected by Len Beadell, but I doubt if it is seen by more than six people in a year. However, one day that humble track may become a main road from Central Australia to Perth. Beadell and his men with mechanical equipment have done a remarkable job in taking the worst bumps out of travel through the area. I'm not sure that I would have liked the trip when Jeremy Long and E. C. Evans were making their first patrols, and fifty miles in a day was considered to be good going. Riding in a vehicle must then have been not too dissimilar to riding a horse in its effect on the spine. Even today much of the road is still suitable only for four-wheel-drive vehicles.

Nosepeg is proud that it passes through his country. He believes that soon it will bring tourists to see the land where he was born. That would not only inflate his pride, but also give him a ready market for his spears. The border, in fact, is Nosepeg's country.

He swept his arm around in a wide arc and announced, 'This is *my* country. Proper good country. I was born at Lake MacDonald — in there.' The dry salt lake was then about twenty miles south of our track.

As a young man — he indicated that he had a beard — Nosepeg left it and walked to Hermannsburg Lutheran Mission station, then the nearest civilization, after his father had been killed in a tribal fight. I have measured the distance on a map and estimate that he walked at least two hundred miles which he dismissed as 'Little-bit-long-way'. At the end of our trip my car was bogged in Derwent Creek and I had to walk ten miles along the road back to Haasts Bluff before being picked up. I thought ten miles was 'Properly-long-way'. Yet walks of two hundred miles and more are not unusual among the nomads, who think nothing of thirty or forty miles during a single day's hunt.

The fight in which Nosepeg's father was killed was one of a series of tribal feuds which were once fought out there between neighbouring tribes. Incredible as it seems, Nosepeg assured me that the tribes fought regularly in hostile country where the simple fact of survival was a constant battle.

He showed me the exact spot near the track where an old man of the Warringari tribe had escaped after being followed for hundreds of miles with Pintubi tribal vengeance on his heels. I can imagine him travelling by day and night, surviving on goannas and rats eaten raw because he would be afraid to light a cooking fire. But his tracks would be indelible in the soft sand and like a beacon pointing the way of his flight to the men on his trail. Then he had reached the stony country which Nosepeg indicated and had been able to eliminate tracks and camouflage his direction. What had he done to cause Pintubi wrath?

'A young Pintubi man died and my people reckon that feller bin "sing" him to death,' Nosepeg said. In other words, the old man had pointed a magic bone at the dead man or in some other way caused a malevolent spirit to enter his body. In the tribes today there remains a fear of the power of these 'Doctor Blackfellows' to induce the death of an enemy by remote control.

In many respects, this was Nosepeg's day. Jugudi the Jagamara had up-staged him yesterday, simply by being found. Now Nosepeg had the front seat again, between Jeremy Long and me. He frequently nudged me in the ribs to draw my attention to points of interest beside the track, loving every minute of riding on four wheels through the country he had first known on two feet. I have no doubt that Nosepeg regarded himself as the most important member of the patrol. As a contributor towards its eventual success, I agree that he was least dispensable.

Nosepeg's name is accurately descriptive. Its origin lies

Peg-Leg Mick lost his right leg in the desert and was carried for four months by another man.

Clothed Pintubi women at Yuendumu. A few years ago they were living naked in the desert.

The first Pintubi found by the 1963 patrol were this woman and child. She borrowed a dress.

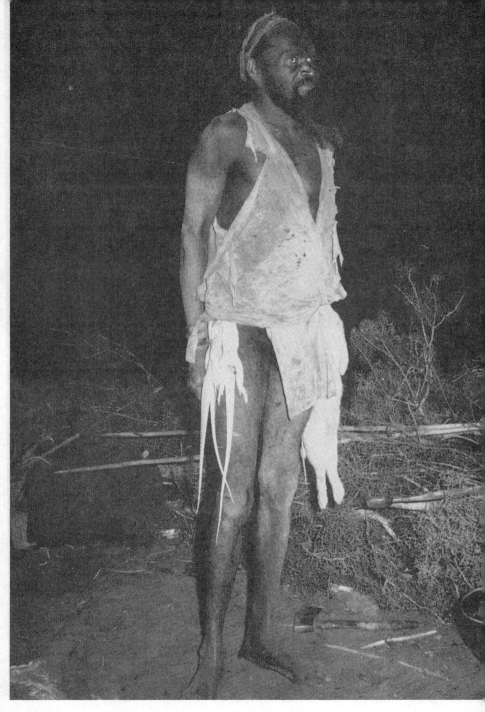

Jugudi. This was how he arrived in camp at dusk with his day's catch — a rabbit and several lizards.

Now look at that for Christmas dinner! Jugudi's small son with a haunch of kangaroo we provided.

Young man at Papunya. A few weeks earlier he was living in the desert, too.

in the fact that when he first entered civilization at Hermannsburg Mission he had a kangaroo bone through his nose. The septum had been pierced in his youth and for many years he wore this tribal decoration.

'I took it out when I went to bed at night, otherwise it got in the way when I turned over,' he said. I've no doubt that this was one of his little jokes.

Nosepeg's kangaroo bone, which he nevertheless carried in his bag, would no longer fit through the hole in his septum. One day he demonstrated, and went on to prove his point by inserting a narrow stick.

'Ah, that's better,' he sighed, as a woman might when relieved of tight shoes.

Nose piercing and decoration is not uncommon among the Pintubi, although I saw only one other man who could wear the bone. I would not be surprised if it was rare, for the pain of a blow on the septum is extremely severe. In the absence of proper tools, piercing is done by the tribesmen with sharpened pieces of wood.

The Sydney anthropologist, M. J. Meggitt, discovered that septum piercing was common among the men of the Wailbri tribe. In his book, *Desert People*, he describes it thus: 'The patient sits with his back against the chest of the operator. This man holds the subject's head firmly in the crook of his arm and, spitting on the fire-hardened point of a thin wand, stabs it sharply through the septum. The brief operation is bloody and painful. The wand, which remains in place until the wound heals in a week or so, is occasionally twisted to prevent it adhering to the scab.' In other tribes the hole is made by a sharpened kangaroo bone.

The agony of such an operation is not difficult to imagine. It is understandable that only the chief stoics among them submit to the primitive surgeon. I'm not sure that I wouldn't prefer the initiation practice of the Gobaboingu tribesmen at Millingimbi, on the north-central coast of Arnhem Land, whose dentists knock out a front tooth of the young men with a wooden chisel and hammer. The patient bites on a piece of wood while this excruciating extraction takes place — to prevent him betraying the unmanly impulse to cry out. Tooth removal is also practised in some desert areas.

Nosepeg had a number of preoccupations as we drove along. Foremost of these was his search for tracks in the red ground and a constant study of the horizon for smoke.

Dingoes, cats, euros and goannas were identified from his seat in the truck as we travelled at thirty miles an hour, often by sign language and accompanied by a dig in the ribs for me to make sure I was awake and understood. At one point he identified the tracks of Jugudi the Jagamara, eighty miles from Sandy Blight Junction where we had last seen them. This time I knew better than to argue.

Jeremy Long then interposed one of his classically laconic statements. 'This is inhabited country,' he said. 'We've been travelling through it all day.'

I could only reply that the inhabitants had plenty of country mixed up with them, for we were to travel two hundred miles without seeing another human being.

Another of Nosepeg's peccadilloes is that he takes snuff, or the aboriginal equivalent of it — he chews pitjuri, a greenish-yellow plant with a mild narcotic effect which they use as tobacco. On the dashboard in front of us he carried a knotted piece of cloth containing his supply of pitjuri (correctly minggulba) previously roasted and rolled in ash. Regularly during the day he opened the rag, took a pinch with his tongue, and chewed on that for a few miles. He then disposed of it, either by dropping it out the window or putting it behind his ear, like chewing gum, to be saved for later.

The tracks we saw most frequently were made by goannas.

Kangaroos and euros were becoming fewer as the mulga opened out into the desert of sandhills and spinifex. The diet of the people who live there consists predominantly of reptiles. Yet I was to discover that these aboriginal men and women do not have the field to themselves in hunting goannas and lizards. They share them with rats — and the rats, of course, need to take care that they are not also eaten by the aborigines. I was astonished one day when Jalyuri, who had been hunting for his living only a few months earlier, said that unusual tracks in the sand that I asked about had been made by a rat dragging a goanna to its hole. He followed the tracks, found the hole, and then began to dig — perhaps just to prove to me that when he said marks were made by a rat dragging a goanna it was really so.

Having observed the uncanny ability of these people to find food and identify human footprints, I was prepared to take his word for it. Nevertheless, Jalyuri insisted on excavating the hole, and a few minutes later produced the remains of a goanna. Half of it had been eaten, obviously by a rat. I was surprised that rats and mice survived at all. One could understand that cats, dogs and larger animals might travel thirty to fifty miles for water, but surely the distances between waterholes would be too great for rodents only a few inches long.

This was a puzzle to which there seemed no solution — until I subsequently read a scientific paper, reprinted from the *Australian Journal of Biological Sciences*, by K. Schmidt-Nielsen and A. E. Newsome, which discussed the water balance in the Mulgara — a carnivorous marsupial mouse living in the Central Australian deserts.

Schmidt-Nielsen and Newsome conducted experiments on Mulgara found near Yuendumu and Papunya. These showed that the mouse does not need to drink. It obtains sufficient water from, and remains in water-balance on, a purely carnivorous diet for indefinite periods.

That night, fifty miles west of the Northern Territory border, in a land where there was almost no water, we substituted with Martinis supplied by Frank Few. What could I do after that apéritif but serve Salt Beef à la Lockwood, garnished with dry biscuits?

Our camp was at Umari, or Old Man and His Wives Rocks, an unusual outcropping of about a dozen pillars of granite, the tallest not more than twelve feet high.

Umari was associated with Tilirungara, a mythical man who strode across the land in pre-history to become one of their Dreamings. Nosepeg said that he began his journey near Mt Liebig, only forty-five miles from Papunya settlement. Having broken tribal commandments, he and his wives, something like Lot's wife, were stricken into pillars of stone.

At a rockhole not far away, which Jalyuri invited us to visit, we were shown a secret rock symbolizing incestuous intercourse between the man and his classificatory mother-in-law. Indentations in the rock were said to represent the knees and the legs of the man and the woman. In tribal eyes, such an offence is an extremely serious crime, for a man is not permitted to speak to or look at his mother-in-law, much less be intimate with her.

In leading us to it, Jalyuri betrayed a certain nervousness with childish laughter, perhaps in an attempt to deprecate his own folly in believing such a fairytale. Nevertheless, I was convinced of his sincerity, though surprised that we should have been taken there. I was astonished when told that I could photograph it. Knowing a little of the sensitivity of the aborigines, I resisted the temptation. Cameras are regarded as sacrilegious in some temples of faith. Who was I to say that this geological manifestation of one of the beliefs of primitive aborigines was any more preposterous than miracles claimed by the proponents of other religions?

Next morning Nosepeg reinstated me as Apprentice Smoke-maker and I soon had a few acres of spinifex burning furiously. Black smoke billowed over the landscape in a graphic message which I thought could not be resisted. But my signals were apparently not heard; at least the telephone at the other end wasn't answered as it had been by Jugudi at Kumanadja rockhole. Perhaps the number was engaged, for Nosepeg, like Jeremy Long, repeatedly insisted that this was inhabited country.

Inhabited by whom? Or what? The only man-tracks we had seen in two hundred miles were Jugudi's. We saw them again that day, more than a hundred miles from his camp at Kumanadja.

'The Jagamara again. He's been here,' Nosepeg said, disinterestedly, as though it was not unusual for a man to be identified so far from where he was last seen.

'Why would he come up here?' I asked.

'He came to get spears,' Nosepeg said.

'Why couldn't he get them at Kumanadja?' I asked.

Nosepeg was out of patience with my stupid questions. The answer was obvious — but I didn't know it. Jeremy Long explained: 'He came here to get the right type of straight acacia for his spear shafts. You'll see them soon; slender trees that are ideal for spear-making.'

We saw a few goanna, dog and cat tracks, but not one kangaroo since leaving Wiyanbiri until we were near Pollock Hills, about a hundred and seventy miles further on. Inhabited country? To nomad aborigines, perhaps it is. But to me it was deserted and desolate, a land depressing in its sameness and its obvious hostility. I knew that if I was stranded there alone I would be dead within a week. In the hot weather, a white man would probably not live more than forty-eight hours.

We were now in heavy sand country and much of our travelling was done in third and lower gears. Twenty miles an hour was a fair speed, but with tours to the north and south of the east-west track our average was much less.

At Winbargu, near a spot which the explorer David Carnegie passed while crossing from Hall's Creek to Coolgardie last century, we made one of these detours to climb Mt Webb.

What a panorama! From the summit of that hill I could see at least fifty miles in all directions. But what could I see? Spinifex, sandhills, stunted trees and little else. I photographed one dead tree, mature and perfectly symmetrical, which was not more than two feet tall. It might have been a thousand years old, having struggled for moisture and life, growing millimetres a year, until finally unequal to the battle with the desert. Its death, like its life, may have been slow and agonizing; I said it was dead but it may still have been dying. That tree was typical of the arrested growth around us. And yet we found the most glorious wild flowers I have seen anywhere, and succulent parakelia on which cattle might fatten — if there had been cattle there to eat it.

On top of Mount Webb, or Winbargu, Nosepeg and Jalyuri began singing the chant appropriate to the country, the liquid language spilling out across the limitless plain, telling of the euro and kangaroo Dreamings which passed that way, lifetimes ago, to the Warburton and Petermann and Musgrave Ranges. The chants had been passed on to the living Pintubi in the only possible way: in the oral tradition of the tribes. They could not write. They could not read. And yet they communicated songs and stories which had not changed since first brought into the desert centuries ago. I printed Nosepeg's name in my notebook, in large block letters. I showed it to him, told him what it was, and asked him to copy it. Although he made his attempt directly beneath mine, copying letter for letter, it was not possible to distinguish the word 'Nosepeg'. This man could read tracks made by his tribesmen in the sand, but he could not read and reproduce his own name. He could sing songs passed on by word of mouth from generation to generation, and tell highly detailed stories tracing the movements of culture heroes across the land. But he could not write, or even copy, a single word.

Nosepeg told me that the Winbargu area was really the tribal country of Arthur Patuta of the Jabanunga skin, the man I met at Yuendumu settlement who had carried Wadi Jugruba of the Jambajimba skin, better known as Peg-Leg Mick, when Mick's leg was injured in a spear fight and eventually fell off.

I'm not surprised that Arthur left there. The wonder is that he stayed as long as he did, until he was a mature man. For the place that he called My Country was almost entirely waterless. Game was scarce. How people managed to live there through the hot summer months while hunting their food was beyond my comprehension.

Why did he leave?

'No kapi,' Nosepeg explained. 'No water.' That was a statement I could well believe. But when he left Arthur went to the Lake Mackay region, which is equally dry. It was not until 1957 when found by the Evans Expedition that Arthur migrated to the east — to the land of taps and gushing water.

I wondered what this country could be used for. Certainly not cattle, even in the sandhills where parakelia grows. Although a succulent high in water content (it is possible to wash one's hands by squeezing a clump of it between the palms) parakelia is treacherous for that very reason. Cattle grazing on it do not need to drink as often, and are inclined to graze well beyond their normal range. The trouble is that in doing so they eat the parakelia, leaving no fluid-rich fodder to sustain them on the way back to water.

If someone invented a commercial use for spinifex or red sand the entire desert would be transformed overnight. They are available in unlimited quantities — many thousands of square miles of both. Given water, much of the red soil could be as productive as the vineyards and citrus groves in the former semi-desert which is now the garden of Sun-raysia around Mildura, Red Cliffs and Renmark. Unfortunately, there is no equivalent of the Murray River flowing through this land. West of Mt Liebig, and until we returned there, I did not see one watercourse which gave promise of being a modest creek after rain. Perhaps when cheap nuclear power is available it may be possible to distil salt water on the northern shore of the Great Australian Bight and pump it into the desert. The distance, after all, is only five hundred miles to Eucla at the head of the Bight. The Eighty Mile Beach, between Broome and Port Hedland, is not much more than three hundred miles away. The pipeline which supplies Kalgoorlie is more than three hundred and fifty miles long.

I am not a geologist, but some who are have already expressed interest in similar country south-west of Alice Springs for its oil-bearing potential. In other parts of the world oil has been found in immense quantities in even poorer deserts — in Texas, Kuwait, Saudi Arabia and the Sahara. I have little doubt that if it should ever be found in the Gibson Desert a way will soon be found to import adequate water. That would mean an undreamed-of transformation. The red land would soon be green.

On our journey, I convinced myself that the entire area was a worthless pan which would never be developed. I tried to think of a use for it other than as the supplier of raw materials for dry sandcastles. Now I have had a pipe-dream and I see it blossoming . . . the tall poppies of oil derricks gushing black gold . . . our track a sealed road . . . Nosepeg the owner of a chain of gas stations at places like Sandy Blight Junction and Jupiter Well . . . Jalyuri as a middleman dealing in stone knives and wooden spears . . . and Hot Dingo stands run by other Pintubi.

Near Winbargu we were taken on a long detour by Jalyuri to find a deposit of quartzite used by the desert men to make their only cutting tool — stone knives. Having bumped over the spinifex clumps for a few miles we asked Jalyuri how much further we had to go. He pointed to a low hill in the middle distance. When we reached that hill he pointed to another equally as far away. I began to believe that the stone knives were a figment of his imagination but finally we came to open ground — with no hill nearby — and found pearl-white fragments sharpened to pin-points and razor-edges on the grindstones of nature. Jalyuri excavated some for us, but he did not appear to be very interested. I got the impression that the stones had ceased to be used. I saw no evidence of them in any of the camps we visited. This paragraph, however, is an important one to me. I had to include it if only because it cost me four hours of discomfort while bumping across spinifex, gibbers and sand to reach the deposit and have this proof of their existence.

On our way we passed through a grove of the acacias known as spear trees. They have a single slender stem, varying from an inch to three inches in diameter at the base, almost no foliage, and tapering ideally for use as spears. This was too much for Nosepeg. He demanded that the vehicles be stopped so that he might abandon us and go off alone to cut the raw material for the nucleus of an arsenal. We picked him up on our return journey — and also his load of pencil-straight timbers which, for the benefit of the botanists, I

renamed Acacia Nosepegii. Jalyuri tore one from the ground,
bit off an unwanted length in his teeth as though it was a
stick of celery, and clamped it in his jaws to straighten it.
This was the beginning of our cargo of sixty-four spears,
some with barbed killing points, which the aborigines made
before we returned to Papunya. The authorities there, without doubt, would regard them as weapons and us as illegal
gun-runners, in spite of Nosepeg's assurances that they were
for the tourist trade. In fact, a spear fight in which several
people were injured broke out at Papunya shortly after these
new weapons arrived, but the damage was done with knives
made from white man's steel.

At our night camp in the Pollock Hills both Nosepeg and
Jalyuri worked late in converting their raw materials into
hand-forged weapons. Jalyuri sometimes used a piece of the
knife-stone he had found earlier in the day as a cutting tool,
but it wasn't difficult to see that he preferred a sharpened
piece of steel which had once been part of a motor-car
spring. Nosepeg straightened the shafts quickly and easily
by placing several inches at a time in hot ashes until the
sap boiled, then taking out the 'kinks' with his knee.

I was surprised to see that Nosepeg was making spears at
all. In fact, I was surprised when he went out to collect
Acacia Nosepegii, because it is not so long ago that he
asked the superintendent of Papunya settlement, where he
lived, to ban or burn all spears. He was a sophisticated man
who had left the ways of the tribes behind him. As an
influential Pintubi he lobbied for others to be made to do
likewise.

'We want to live like whitefellers, not a mob of myall
blackfellers,' he explained. 'All that spear business is
finished.'

The spears were actually collected, and sold to tourists
or destroyed as the old man wished. I suppose this came

under the heading of Disarmament. It could even be said that a test-ban treaty was signed by the warring nations — the Pintubi, the Wailbri, the Kukutja, the Pitjantjara — and the United Nations arbitrator, represented by the settlement superintendent. I have often wondered who got most of the money from the sale of the spears. I asked Nosepeg, who hid behind the kind of smile that the novelists like to call 'enigmatic', but which plainly suggested that the transaction was not without profit to him. After all, when armaments are being sold it is inevitable that someone's bank manager will smile.

But the Pintubi have not yet ceased to be hunting men or warlike men. Only a few months after this treaty was negotiated the spear-trees were being cut again, and Nosepeg was one of the first to acquire a new armoury of Stone Age weapons. I think he is just an incurable 'gun-runner'. However, as an individual I'm sure that he cannot dictate the habits of the nomads as a group. If they want to fight with spears, what Nosepeg thinks about it won't weigh too heavily with them. As has been demonstrated, he can't even dictate successfully to himself.

On our way back from the Stone-Knife Place to the 'main' road, Jalyuri sat in the cabin with Long and me, ostensibly to show us a 'short cut'. Like other short cuts I have known, it turned out to be the long way around. He couldn't speak one word of English; however, I know, even in Pintubi, when I'm travelling in the wrong direction; before we had gone far I began insisting that we should be travelling the opposite way.

Jalyuri did not understand what I said and Jeremy Long, who was driving, preferred the Pintubi's directions to mine. He had been with them often enough to realize that if an aboriginal who could never be lost in his own country

wanted to travel south when our path lay north, there must
be a good reason for it.

We bumped around the ends of sandhills and found gaps
through others, but eventually we reached a cul-de-sac in
the sand that was obviously impassable. And there it was
that I discovered Jalyuri's insistence on the long diversion
was not without reason. He led us on foot for a few hundred
yards to the end of this blind alley in the dunes. Behind one
of them we came upon an extraordinary group of limestone
outcrops; perhaps as many as a hundred pinnacles, none of
them more than three feet high, but each perfect in its
separateness. This was a remarkable geological formation.
In the midst of sandhills we found a conglomeration of limestone! I was not surprised, as with other distinctive features
like Old Man and His Wives Rocks, when Jalyuri said
repeatedly: 'Mamu! Mamu! Mamu!' which was interpreted
as the name of a mythical woman who had come there and
been given eternal life in the limestone. The place was now
a sacred Dreaming, a totemic centre of great significance in
the tribal culture. Jeremy Long was convinced that we were
the first white men ever to have been there, either by
accident or invitation. It was all most impressive, especially
as Jalyuri repeated reverently and constantly: 'Mamu!
Mamu!'

It is not clear whether aborigines in this area observe the
Earth Mother cult common to the Roper River, eastern
Arnhem Land and East Kimberley tribes. Some anthropolo-
gists believe they do, but others are convinced they do not.
They have had such infrequent contact, and that only in
recent years, that little is known of their culture. But it did
seem apparent from Jalyuri's invocation of Mamu's name
that they subscribe to a cult in which a mythical woman
figures significantly. I came away as from a place of worship;
a cathedral of paganism, to be sure, like Umari — but with-

Jugudi's family eating kangaroo meat we gave them. It may have been the most food they'd seen.

Jalyuri (left) and Nosepeg examining tracks. They were able to name the people who made them.

Patrol Leader Jeremy Long discusses tactics with Nosepeg, our chief interpreter, and Tim.

Nosepeg and Jalyuri making wooden spears at a night-camp. They returned with about sixty.

Bush wireless! A smoke signal hangs on the horizon. It was ours, sent from the top of nearby Mt Webb

Umari, or Old Man and His Wives Rocks, an aboriginal 'dreaming place' near the N.T.-W.A. border.

This was how we communicated. Nosepeg makes our first spinifex fire for black signal smoke, seen for 20 miles.

out doubt a temple, a mosque, a josshouse or a shrine in the religious life of the Pintubi. Unlike our churches, it did not have a spire. It did not stand on a hill or advertise its presence with a carillon. I was not asked to take off my shoes, though Jalyuri was barefooted. We walked up the steps of sand and desecrated the edifice itself by walking all over it. Yet there was no hint of reproof in Jalyuri's manner; on the contrary, he walked nonchalantly on the pillars himself, while failing to disguise the depth of his reverence.

For the first few days of our journey from Papunya, Nosepeg was star-boarder, chief cook, interpreter, and self-appointed film star. He posed at the drop of a lens hood, and let it be widely known that he had once been to Sydney to take part in a television film about Central Australia. On that occasion, at Sydney airport, he caused a little consternation by taking his clothes off for the benefit of cameramen and appearing cnly in a loin cloth. He would have had to be asked only once to take that off, too. When we met desert aborigines and the cameras were whirring Nosepeg was never far from centre-stage. On several occasions he suggested poses of himself, and some of them showed a keen appreciation of the needs of photography. Without flash-bulbs it is difficult to photograph an aboriginal face successfully while in shadow. When Nosepeg was in front of a shutter he made sure his face was in sunlight. He volunteered one excellent shot of himself sucking honey from the flower-spike of a grevillea bush.

After a few days, however, he began to be up-staged by Jalyuri the Primitive, a natural actor who had probably never seen a film and certainly did not know any of the technical facts associated with cameras or photography. But he had obviously acted in enough tribal corroborees to understand what was required of him for moving film. His appearance was spoilt by a dirty coat he wore day and night, a horrible navy pin-stripe which had once belonged to a winter suit. It was only faintly removed from the colour of the red dirt around us, and looked out of place on his back. This was common to all the Pintubi we met; in their natural state they had an innate dignity, though completely naked. The moment they tried to wear cast-off clothes that was destroyed and their appearance suffered. Jalyuri didn't mind removing his coat, but he did mind the effort involved. Once he got the thing on he wanted it to stay there. He was still unpractised in the subtle art of getting his arms into the sleeves. Whereas taking a coat off and putting it on again is a simple matter for men who are used to it, to Jalyuri it was a major exercise, to be approached as an undertaking requiring considerable skill and effort. However, when it was off he was a different man, especially as he also removed a shirt and singlet which were filthier than mine.

For the first time, he showed magnificent cicatrices on his chest and arms — heavily raised scars inflicted in the fires of tribal initiation — and the barrelled torso of an exceptional physique developed by years of walking and hunting in the desert. As a young man, Jalyuri lay on his back one night, on a primitive corroboree ground, while the appropriate relative cut him deeply across the chest and down the upper-arms, perhaps with one of the very stone knives we had found that day, for they had no steel or tin. He lay there patiently until blood coagulated in and around the wound, forming scar tissue over which the skin would eventually grow. In most tribes these cicatrices are filled with ashes or down to give the raised effect, but when questioned by Nosepeg, Jalyuri insisted that ashes were not used on him. In some areas they are inflicted by tribal friends or distant relatives who have no thought of decorating the man's body; their rather more selfish impulse is that they will be remembered throughout his life by the man thus decorated. I have seen scars which, if on my body, would certainly make me remember the artist for all time, but not with gratitude or affection. Jalyuri's cicatrices, however, were among the neatest and most decorative I have seen. A master-surgeon equipped with fine instruments could not have improved on the simple design of double lines crossed in the centre by a transverse band. It seemed apparent that among the Pintubi, as with the Arnhemlanders and other northern tribes, cicatrices are not a compulsory part of initiation ceremonies, but voluntary marks produced during a penance the man could either accept or reject when approached by one who wanted to cut him. Jugudi, who bore a remarkable physical resemblance to Jalyuri, was similarly marked. But other tribesmen we found were not. This seems to indicate free choice in the matter.

One other incident made me think that Nosepeg might feel his stardom being threatened, or that he would have to share star billing. One night I went to their camp to ask permission to photograph spear-making, and Frank Few was anxious to get the sequence in his film. This was granted without demur. When filming began Jalyuri again removed his coat, shirt and singlet. But Nosepeg removed his trousers also and posed quite naked.

'No girls out here,' he said. Not that it would have mattered much if there had been, for those we saw were naked themselves and accompanied by naked men. Nakedness is a way of life to these people. They have never known any other. That being so, they have none of the prudery, none of the shame, and none of the embarrassment which would be felt by Europeans in similar circumstances.

For two days we had splendid fun in the mild sunshine, bumping over fifty thousand clumps of spinifex to see stone knives in the place where they were mined, and to collect

Acacia Nosepegii and watch the manufacture of pointed and barbed wooden spears. But I began to worry that we weren't seeing other aborigines, although we had seen their tracks and their smoke on numerous occasions. After all, we were in what Jeremy Long had described as 'inhabited country'. I wanted to see more of the inhabitants.

Long proposed that next day we would leave the Pollock Hills area and perhaps reach Jupiter Well, 540 miles west of Alice Springs, for our next camp. We were all very dirty, and looked forward to a bath at the well. This pleasure, however, was to be delayed for several more days, for Apprentice Smoke-Maker Lockwood had his first telephone call from Inland Space that evening. A fire we made at Mt Webb was answered with a thin black spiral in the southern sky. Nosepeg and Jalyuri pointed to it and confirmed that it was made by aborigines. Near Mamu they had also seen and identified tracks they said were made by a man of the Jabangadi skin who was once a stockman on the Canning stockroute, but retired from that kind of work to re-enter the desert as a nomadic hunter.

How they knew the tracks belonged to him was an insoluble mystery to me, for they seemed to be days old and windblown. But I doubted them not. Hadn't I seen Nosepeg examine a track near Kumanadja and pronounce at once, 'The Jagamara'?

The Jagamara it had been. My scepticism had vanished.

The moon that night was never brighter. Seen from the Gibson Desert, I didn't wonder that astronauts wanted to reach it, to closely inspect a floating white neon which bathed in beauty with light it did not itself possess an otherwise ugly and inhospitable land more than two hundred thousand miles away. The countless stars seemed more infinite, and yet somehow easier to count. The desert stillness could be felt. The loudest noise was made by the wings of flies and the crackle of campfire flames. There were few birds — an occasional hawk, a flock of finches when we were near water, and one or two wagtails.

By day the desert had impressed me as sterile country, but in the moonlight it was fertile with extravagant beauty which began with the sunsets. I could see the horizon spinning towards the enormous sun, shrouded in a backdrop of bright pink sky. Our view of it was seldom broken by trees on the skyline and never by buildings. Out here, in fact, it was possible to see all the way to the setting sun, as though across an ocean. The curvature of the earth was the nearest landmark.

Jalyuri and Nosepeg were unaware of the beauty surrounding them, and would have been unimpressed if I had drawn their attention to it. To them, there is beauty only in fat goannas and desert rats and euros, for which they were preparing their spears — although they wouldn't eat bush food, apart from rich red kangaroo meat, while plenty of flour was available for damper. Nosepeg often made a meal of damper spread thickly with sweetened condensed milk, the sight of which was enough to upset me.

'Number One tucker!' he said when I asked if he liked the stuff.

We had much better fare: a curry I made with salt beef, tinned vegetables, potatoes and onions, and a fair amount of grit I accidentally kicked into the pot. Not one of our party complained, for the apparent reason that they knew I would quit as cook at the first derogatory comment about my incredible concoctions. Sometimes these were revolting, but they were eaten stoically by men who either had ravenous appetites and jaded palates or utterly detested the thought of having to cook for themselves.

I hadn't washed for three days or shaved for a week, but I had invented curry-flavoured toothpaste. My wet toothbrush somehow became coated and impregnated with curry powder.

Ah, well. It's not bad, at that. There are worse things than a curry nightcap.

Tracks Without Men

Jeremy Long is a man who cannot resist either smoke signals or human tracks. To him, they are like homing beacons. He follows them without thought of comfort for himself or discomfort for his friends. Generally they lead to what he is looking for — primitive aborigines. I'm sure they figure more significantly in his life than in that of any other living white man; both have led him into some odd corners of an odd desert, and I'll be surprised if they don't continue to do so for further years, or at least until all the Pintubi have been brought into settlements and ration depots. When that happens there will probably be word of tribes elsewhere; perhaps the rumours we have often heard of improbable nomads hiding in the Stone Country of Arnhem Land, inside the almost impenetrable escarpments, will be substantiated. Then he'll be off again to find their smokes and their tracks.

Having been sidetracked by the detours to Mamu and the Stone-Knife Place, we camped near Pollock Hills when we might have been many miles nearer to our goal at Jupiter Well. But we were to be there yet another night after our experts, Nosepeg and Jalyuri, had evaluated the significance of the tracks we saw near Mamu and the black spiral of smoke in the southern sky.

Jeremy now proposed that instead of going on to Jupiter Well we should set out across country for the people who were answering our call. That might mean anything from twenty to fifty miles over sandhills and spinifex, but distance and discomfort were unimportant when the main chance was involved: contact with people.

Where the highways are, twenty or fifty miles might mean a one-hour detour. But it is a very different matter in the Gibson Desert. Jeremy's decision meant hours, perhaps days, of spinifex-bashing. We would jolt along at five miles an hour with heavy loads of petrol, water and food on both vehicles, while we watched the ground and the sky for other signs of habitation.

Nor could we travel at five miles an hour in a straight line. That would have meant twenty miles in four hours, which we might have regarded as average going. But between us and that smoke were serried sandhills, some of them ten miles long. Crossing them was fraught with danger even when we could find low 'saddles', which wasn't always possible, so they had to be skirted. Jeremy estimated that our speed, in these circumstances, could be reduced to ten miles a day in a direct line towards the smoke. That meant at least two days to reach the nomads, unless they saw our approaching smokes and took the risk of leaving water to walk towards us. Their speed on foot would probably be twice ours, and perhaps more, but the desert men have learnt by fearful experience to consider carefully before going too far away from water. So I fixed my saddle in position and prepared for a day or so of bucking vehicles.

Nosepeg began the day by setting fire to a few acres of mulga. An hour later Apprentice Lockwood was very proud of himself when he was first to discover answering smoke on the horizon, and excitedly pointed it out. It seemed to be not more than ten miles away.

Nosepeg looked at me with withering scorn and spat expressively. Jalyuri the nomad had not risen from his seat at the campfire; that had puzzled me, but I regarded it as a fortuitous circumstance which had made possible my discovery of the signal in the south. Now he pointed to Nosepeg's smoke, then to mine on the horizon, and indicated with sign-talk that they were one and the same. Nosepeg's smoke had drifted and been held low by the cool morning air. It was fool's gold.

'Poor old man, you properly blind along your eye,' Nosepeg said.

After that episode, he made it obvious that I would need many more lessons before graduating in his esteem as a Journeyman Smoke-Maker. I was miserably crestfallen, not only because I made a fool of myself but also because my false alarm meant spine-bashing of the most literal kind; the day was spent crossing sandhills and spinifex flats.

Nosepeg must have expected action that morning. He sat on the back of the truck rather than in the cabin, a change he made only when he wanted a more elevated, less interrupted view of the horizon. We had been travelling for not more than an hour when Nosepeg banged urgently on the roof. He had seen tracks among the spinifex only fifteen yards from our path. He and Jalyuri examined them briefly and identified them instantly.

They were, he said, the tracks of three Pintubi women of the Nangala, Nabaljari and Naburula skins. There were three children with them, the footprints of one of which was positively identified as belonging to a boy whose mother had died a year earlier.

Nosepeg and Jalyuri did this just as easily as I might identify my wife's voice or one of her dresses. They did not appear to make a close or detailed inspection of the tracks. Jalyuri, especially, gave them scant attention, and yet it seemed to me that Nosepeg deferred to him in at least this one matter where expert opinion was invaluable.

The tracks, unfortunately, were estimated to be a week old. How that could be decided when there had been daily winds to disturb the outlines also puzzled me. Moreover, the women were moving east, the direction from which we had come. They were back there somewhere, probably south of our track.

In any case, we would have to leave them until our return journey, or until Jeremy Long made another patrol. We now had to get on to our objective — the smoke in the southern sky which hadn't been repeated since we first saw it. Why that was so was another enigma. I know that if I wanted to attract attention in the desert, knowing that other human beings were nearby, I would become an incendiarist-extraordinary. These people, on the other hand, had adjusted their dampers so that no smoke rose.

We crossed the first big sandhill without trouble, without having to unload any of our gear. The plain to the next one was about five miles wide, and dotted with spinifex bushes often two feet tall. Again I thought what a pity it was that a commercial use had not been found for this hardy plant, often lushly green after years of drought, growing in prickled clumps from one foot to five in diameter — and millions upon millions of them. Stock will eat the seed stalks and the seeds, too, when other fodder is unavailable. I have heard pastoralists discussing the possibility of harvesting the seeds and using them as oats; the trouble is that they'd probably have to cover a square mile to get a bagful.

Jalyuri sat in the cabin with us and unerringly pointed the way to a gap in the next sandhill which neither Long nor I could see until we were within two hundred yards of it. This led into a narrow gulch — a very dry one which reminded me of all the Death Valleys I'd ever read about. In early August, a normally cool month, the basin formed by the dunes was uncomfortably hot for my winter clothes. What the heat in there would be like in January is best left to the imagination. My guess is that the average would be between 150 and 180 degrees. There is no shade, so these are sun temperatures. I doubt if even the hardy nomads could live there for many hours without water. Actually the basin contained a waterhole, or a soak, but it was dry. Jalyuri had led us to it through a gap in sandhills we didn't know existed and couldn't see until almost on top of it. He knew exactly where he was. So did I: we were west of Alice Springs and east of the Indian Ocean.

Daily association had made Jalyuri seem less a wild man than when I first met him at Papunya. There, among civilized and semi-civilized men and women from other tribes, he represented the Stone Age. His forehead was bound with a red grass string. At the back of his head, forming a bun, he wore a cloth bag tied with fibre in which he carried his few valuables. Anyone wanting to steal it would have to cut off his hair or his head. As the days in the desert passed, however, I became accustomed to his appearance and manner and thought of him as just another aboriginal. But my values were re-adjusted by an incident which showed without doubt that he still lived in another world. At one of our stops I got out of the vehicle and shut the door. A few minutes later Jalyuri wanted to get out, too, but he had no idea how to do so. He tried pushing the door open. When that didn't succeed he attempted to lift it off its hinges. I explained by sign-talk that he had to turn the handle. This was an operation that he was apparently incapable of performing. He did not understand that the handle depressed a tongue in the door which fitted into a groove on the door-pillar, allowing it to open. He therefore believed it should be possible to open the door either by pushing or lifting it. The superintendent of Yuendumu settlement, Alex Bishaw, told me that one of the most difficult lessons for all the Pintubi when they first came out of the desert was to open and shut doors in buildings. They were utterly mysti-

fied by round knobs which had to be turned, and would have
perished inside if required to let themselves out.

Yet I had no illusions as to whose intellect was superior
in the desert where there are no doors to open: no refrigerator doors, no pantry doors, no cupboard doors. The key to
the door of life out there unlocked only a man's ability to
track and hunt game. I knew that in this country Jalyuri
would survive by his wits and live to old age. I would perish
in a week or so. I did not have his stamina. I did not have
trained eyes to tell me which holes secreted fat goannas. I
did not have women with yam sticks to dig tubers from the
baked soil and gather berries from desert bushes.

Jalyuri continued to direct us with his hands through the
maze of sandhills, opening up other valleys and gulches and
taking us to other dry waterholes. I don't know how he
found any of them, for one part of the country appeared to
me to be identical with any other part. At one dry hole,
named Mandangundja, Jalyuri climbed into a shallow cave
which held the bones of a kangaroo, but there was no
evidence of water having been present for a long time. We
saw rabbit warrens, however, and ample proof that cattle
could live if artificial water was provided with sub-artesian
bores. There were extensive patches of the parakelia I have
spoken about. Cattle were not present here because there
were no white men. We were assuredly the first party ever to
visit the area — in fact, everywhere we travelled in this
desert off the main track we could be confident of being the
first to see it other than aborigines. I have been in most
corners of Australia, but never have I seen so much virgin
country.

A day earlier, Jeremy Long wore a compass on his wrist
when we climbed a mountain. He wanted it to give him an
accurate north and south while map-reading.

Natural food wasn't replaced entirely by ours. Anatjari's son, Wili, eating a small lizard.

One of Anatjari's daughters blows on her own small fire to make a blaze for warmth at night.

Like his daughters (above) Anatjari was soon addicted to damper. Jeremy Long at left.

Mountain Devil (Moloch Horridus). A few of these and two truffles were the only food Yaliti had.

Nim-Nim gets water in a pitchi from a 10-foot deep hole. Wet sand (top left) was scooped out as level dropped.

But on this day he didn't bother; to find his way around the country we were now in he would never swap an aboriginal for a compass, especially one of Jalyuri's calibre who knew it intimately, having used hundreds of square miles of it as his hunting ground.

'When you are looking for waterholes or trying to find a path through sandhills there is no substitute for a tribesman with local knowledge," Long said.

I believed him. Jalyuri continued to prove it by leading us through a series of really treacherous dunes where the sand must almost bubble and boil in summer.

He also took us back safely. I was lost, but he was at home. I suspect that once or twice he laughed at me for so patently not knowing where I was.

In revenge, I've promised myself that one day I will take him to Melbourne and Sydney. I'll be interested to see how he shapes at Young and Jackson's corner and King's Cross during the peak traffic hour. I'd love to see him sitting there on the footpath, hopelessly lost, trying to sustain himself by digging a goanna from a storm drain as he did from a dry hole at Jindara, grabbing it by the tail, knocking it once on the back of the head with a stick, and later eating it for supper, tail, head and all. He would starve with restaurants all around him, and thirst on a pub corner, not knowing where to spend the few shillings that would buy him food and drink.

The smoke we had seen in the southern sky promised us an exciting and interesting day with Stone Age Pintubi. Instead, it was to be a frustrating one.

We saw tracks but no more smoke. Several dry waterholes to which Jalyuri led us had not been visited by aborigines for a long time.

Nosepeg was noticeably disappointed, having been

deprived of his role in the limelight as chief interpreter. I was just sore. We had bumped over the spinifex for seven hours without reward.

Imagine a highway strewn with stacks of sand and grass eighteen inches to two feet high at intervals of one yard and travelling over it all day in a four-wheel-drive vehicle. If you can do that you will have some idea of what the ride was like.

We returned to our previous camp on the ground at Pollock Hills, but I thought we were fortunate to be back at all. Frank Few and Jeremy Long had fixed a broken-down engine when the nearest mechanic was at Papunya, three hundred miles away.

Nosepeg's explanation of our inability to find the makers of the previous day's smoke was that they had run away.

He said they must have realized the smoke-makers at our end included white men, which was true, and that they did not want to meet us.

It might seem incredible that people living on goannas and other bush food should run away from flour, tea and sugar. I thought they would have hurried in to meet us. Nosepeg had an answer for that, too.

'They're frightened,' he said.

'Who are they frightened of?'

'You,' he said. 'Any whitefeller.'

'Why?' I had imagined that the days had gone forever when aborigines were afraid of white men, although I knew they had been given adequate reason for such fear in the past.

Nosepeg made the sign of the handcuffs — crossed wrists.

'Too much belting,' he said. 'It was a long time ago, but these people have heard the stories and they're frightened.'

I asked if these people would have heard of the Coniston massacre, the disgraceful episode in 1928 when a total of

thirty-one aborigines were admitted to have been shot dead
by white men, including a policeman, who went into the
desert about three hundred miles north-east of our position
on a punitive expedition. They shot seventeen men and
women in one camp and fourteen in another thirty miles
away — and said it was done in self-defence because the
natives attacked them with spears. A Commission of Inquiry
was appointed and evidence taken from thirty witnesses over
a period of six months. The Commission found no evidence
to support the suggestion of a 'punitive' expedition and said
the shootings were justified. One witness told the Commission that the shooting of a number of women was 'uninten-
tional and accidental'. In the same district a few years later
another Commission of Inquiry was necessary to investigate
allegations of malpractice after a pastoralist had been
acquitted on a charge of trussing an aboriginal with a leather
surcingle and beating him with sticks. There was the case,
not far away, of an aboriginal woman who was chained by
the neck to the stirrup iron of a horse and made to walk like
that for seventy miles. She cried for water and became ill
with dysentery. When she could no longer walk she was
dragged along on her belly. At one night-camp she was
chained upright to a tree. In the morning she was dead.
An aboriginal man who had stolen food had a rope tied
around his neck and attached to the rear of a truck. He was
then made to run behind the vehicle — until the speed
became too fast and his head was dragged off.

Episodes like these are still remembered vividly by the
tribesmen. A few days before leaving for the Pintubi country
I interviewed survivors of the Coniston massacre at a cattle
station near Yuendumu. More than thirty years after it happened, they still did not want to talk about it. I went to see
those men in an attempt to establish whether there was any

link between the massacres and other cruelties and the fact that Pintubi tribesmen had remained in the desert, apparently avoiding contact with Europeans.

But they belonged to a different tribe—the Anmatjira—and did not know whether these events had influenced the Pintubi.

Now I was in their tribal country, with a tribesman who spoke my language telling me plainly that they were frightened—that there had been 'too much belting'. I thought that at last I might be able to establish a link between the massacres and tribal fear. I asked him if his tribesmen had heard about the killings at Coniston.

'I know about them, but these desert people have never heard those stories,' he said.

Nor did they know about One-Arm Ngugudi Juburula, who had lost an arm which grew gangrenous inside a ratchet handcuff. His whitefeller name of Paddy Handcuffs is a terrible indictment of our treatment of these soft-spoken, witty, self-reliant men—the men I would desperately want to know if the time should ever come when tribes they've never heard of started throwing hydrogen-headed spears at one another. In their company, sharing their ability to live off the land, I would have a better-than-evens chance of survival.

The tragedy of missing the Pintubi group we had chased across the sandhills, from my point of view, was that they had never had contact with European society. I would gladly have given Paddy Handcuffs my spare arm if, in return, I might have had the privilege of meeting these relatives of his who had not seen white skin. But they were frightened . . . they fled in the opposite direction and were soon fifty miles away.

'They didn't even light cooking fires,' Nosepeg said.

'What about that smoke we saw?' I asked.

'That was put up before they knew whitefellers were with us. They found that out and they gone to buggery.' (Nosepeg had several measures of distance: Close-up, Little-bit-long-way, Long-way, and Gone-to-buggery. We knew, when he referred to the last measure, that it was too far for us.)

On our way back to Pollock Hills we recrossed the tracks of the three women and their children who were travelling east. Nosepeg had told me earlier that one of the children was an orphan. Now he told me the truly terrible story of the child's father, Windaru Jangala, the man who died in the confined dead-end of a cave which admitted him when he followed porcupine tracks into the furthest chamber, but held him there, unable to turn or to squeeze his buttocks back through the narrow passage, until he perished on his hands and knees.

The Gibson Desert is a hostile place, and the manner of death is sometimes harrowing in the extreme. But I could imagine none tougher than Windaru Jangala's in a dark hole in the desert floor.

Anatjari . . .
And His Stone Age Wives

Jalyuri and Nosepeg, working late at night, had seven perfectly matched spears to show us in the morning. That number was to grow to more than sixty before the trip ended. The other aboriginal who had stayed with us when our party was divided at Kumanadja, Snowy Jambajimba, showed no interest at all in the manufacture of these weapons. I think he regarded it as a job for primitives. Although Nosepeg certainly did not belong to that category —on the contrary, he was an extremely sophisticated man— Snowy put himself in a higher social caste. He was well dressed. He was, moreover, a qualified motor driver—a fact which did not prevent me feeling some moments of insecurity when he took our heavily laden vehicle through deep sand. His reflexes seemed slower than Jeremy Long's when the rear wheels began sliding. I had visions of being burnt to death beneath exploding petrol drums.

The sharpened wooden tips of Jalyuri's and Nosepeg's spears, hardened in fire, were designed to penetrate the toughest kangaroo hides. But there seemed to me to be one weakness in their industry: they had more spears than kangaroos. For three days we had not seen an animal bigger than a goanna and I appreciated, more than ever, that any man who could stay alive and support a family in that country was a genius.

Our track was still due west. Occasionally it turned to skirt the ends of sandhills, but for no other reason. We had now come five hundred miles from Alice Springs, and were a hundred and fifty miles inside Western Australia. In the three hundred and fifty miles from Papunya settlement we had seen just one group of Pintubi — Jugudi and his family of two wives and two children at Kumanadja rockhole — and they were two hundred miles behind us.

'Inhabited country!' Jeremy Long had said. I'm sure my voice carried a heavier load of scorn each time I repeated the phrase — and I did so regularly, for I was determined not to let him forget.

It was becoming strikingly beautiful country with a multiplicity of wild flowers that reminded me of Walt Disney's film, *The Living Desert.* Here at last, I thought, was a practical use for the land: the wild flowers I saw in a few acres would be worth hundreds of pounds in city florists' shops. And there was far more than a few acres; in fact there were hundreds of thousands of brilliantly blooming acres — a country come alive with many varieties of flannel flower, grevillea, purple wax and heather, and dozens that I could not identify. The grevillea was so luscious that Nosepeg ate honey dripping from blooms twelve inches long. One could have a factory to refine and can natural honey, by-passing the bees as unnecessary middlemen. But it's contrary country, and I would not wish to be first to try taming it. Never a running watercourse of any kind, and seldom so much as a dry creek bed. In some places, in the midst of exotic wildflowers, the Acacia Nosepegii was dead, or drooping so badly that Nosepeg and Jalyuri were not interested; straightening those shafts would have been a major undertaking.

This desert is at once beautiful and ugly. The sandhills and the spinifex and stunted desert bushes remained; yet

the leavening of secondary growth, of these areas of durable
perennials, made it seem that the uninhabitable desert was
at last inhabited. Jeremy Long had been right, after all, and,
as immediate events were to prove, in other than botanical
respects.

Our dinner-camp that day was adjacent to sandhills in the
vicinity of Likilnga waterhole, where we believed that contact would be made with a nomadic family. There was
evidence that at least seven people had been there recently,
but now they were gone — and we didn't know where.
However, this was to be only a temporary frustration.
Jalyuri and Nosepeg ran true to form by naming every
person whose tracks they examined — two men, two women
and three children. They were wrong in one item: the second
man, as it turned out, was really a fourteen-year-old boy,
although he had large feet.

The tracks were fresh, and we felt convinced that people
must be living nearby. Why hadn't they answered our
smoke? It was all extremely perplexing.

I wondered if we were being shadowed. Were groups of
aborigines who did not want to know us watching and
following us stealthily from behind the maze of sandhills?
Had they, too, heard the stories of cruelty, of white man's
inhumanity to black man, and decided not to look upon our
hot faces?

Our luck was to change dramatically within an hour.

Instead of eating lunch, Jalyuri walked north across the
sandhills with Snowy Jambajimba, apparently without con-
sulting Nosepeg, who stayed with us.

Such an act was quite out of character for Jalyuri, who
normally preferred to curl up on the ground and go to sleep.
There was no smoke to guide or influence him, yet he must

have known instinctively that tribesmen of his were within easy walking distance. I thought it even more out of character that Jalyuri and Snowy had not returned to the vehicles by the time we were ready to leave. It was thought possible that they may have walked along the dunes and rejoined our track a few miles to the westward, though I could not imagine why they should have done that. I knew that neither of those men liked walking merely for the sake of exercise.

We left the camping spot and drove two or three miles without them. When they did not appear near the track we had no choice but to go back and contain our patience while waiting for them to return at their leisure. I was still puzzled by this extraordinary behaviour.

Jeremy Long and I climbed the nearest sandhill to see the view on the other side, expecting that we would see nothing more than other sandhills. This wasn't so; descending the dune across the valley in front of us were Jalyuri and Snowy. Both were pointing northward, and Jalyuri made the clenched-fist sign for 'Man'. We knew then that before long, unless they had run away, we would see the desert people we had driven five hundred miles to find, people who, perhaps had never seen white men.

And so it proved.

Jalyuri and Snowy joined us. Snowy explained that they had found a family group at a waterhole only a short distance from Likilnga. He said the group comprised a man, his two wives and three children. A small boy had run away when told that strangers wearing clothes were near.

That accounted for only six, although seven sets of tracks had been identified. Where was the other man?

Jeremy Long decided to take the vehicles across the sandhills to the waterhole. As we walked back towards them,

Jalyuri pointed again and there, far away, we saw the lone figure of a hunting man, not more than one hundred yards from the trucks. He had come down from the ridges south of our track; I wondered again whether he had kept us under observation while we rested there at lunchtime.

When we were still a hundred yards from him he stopped and stood quite still, resting on his spear and yam stick. Jalyuri went ahead to the vehicles, took damper and tinned meat from a tucker box and approached him, without any greeting I could hear, with food in his hands. The stranger took it and began to eat instantly. I doubt if he had ever had two kinds of food at once in his life; later we had to show him how to spread the meat on his damper.

This lone figure in the desert was a fourteen year old boy of the Jambajimba skin. He was extremely thin, but not suffering noticeably from malnutrition although he had every right to be: he had been hunting all day without food or water, and with nothing to show for it.

His body was coated with red sand and his abdomen scarred with burns inflicted by firesticks he carried too closely in the cold weather. This was a condition common to all the people we found: the abdomens of some of them were as much pink as black. They also suffered severely from burns sustained in campfires they rolled into at night. That didn't surprise me, for they slept almost on top of the fires.

There is, however, another reason for body scarring. It is graphically illustrated by the man I think of as the leading authority on the Aranda tribe, Mr. T. G. H. Strehlow, M.A.

Strehlow was born at Hermannsburg, eighty miles west of Alice Springs, where his father was an early Lutheran missionary. He became fluent in the Aranda language and understood the tribal life and customs with an intimacy not possible for anyone who was not bilingual. In a booklet entitled *Nomads in No-Man's-Land,* Strehlow makes this further interesting point on the subject of body burns:

'Only after passing through . . . painful initiation rites were Aranda youths able to achieve the full social status of initiated men; and only initiated men were permitted to marry and to be introduced into the aboriginal spiritual world of myth and sacred tradition. These were the high rewards, whose prospect emboldened the youths to face up to the grim ordeals of their manhood rites. All boys deliberately trained themselves to bear pain with composure for years before the time came for them to undergo initiation.

'When I was still a boy at Hermannsburg, one of the favourite pastimes for children of both sexes from the age of about eight till the years of puberty consisted in picking up live coals from the campfires and placing them on their own bare arms and legs. They were left on the bare skin until they had lost their glow. Courage was assessed according to the child's ability to bear this self-inflicted torture without flinching and sometimes even with unconcerned laughter.

'The proudest child at the campfire would be the one who had endured the biggest burn from the largest live coal picked out of the fire. In this way all children learnt that there are limits even to pain — that a point is reached beyond which pain cannot go, and that it is possible, in many cases, for a trained person to come close to this limit of pain without disgracing himself by crying out aloud.

'This element of pain was a vital ingredient of the initiation ritual. For in addition to providing a gateway to marriage and an introduction to the spiritual world, the manhood rites had the important social purposes of inculcating respect for authority of the elders of each local group, and of ensuring the dutiful submission of all men to the

traditional social controls and to the norms of conduct which
have been popularly termed "tribal laws".'

The Jambajimba boy, named Nim-Nim, wore only a brief
loin cloth tied around his waist with a string. He was the son
of a man who had perished in the desert about two years
earlier and was being cared for by his tribal brother, the man
Jalyuri and Snowy had seen. He was about five feet seven
inches tall and I estimated his weight at not more than six
and a half stones. He had a pleasant, friendly face, with a
perpetual smile that disclosed brilliant white teeth. Within
a few minutes he lost all his initial shyness, and for the next
week was to be like a shadow to us. He soon made himself
at home in our camp and on our vehicles. Unfortunately, he
did not understand when told to go away, which eventually
became a little trying. I don't want to have to live with my
closest friends all the time, let alone strange youths who
can't speak my language, nor I theirs. However, he was
friendly and likeable, and his smile was a pleasant contrast
to the glum, unhappy faces of men and women we found
several days later.

Since leaving Papunya, Jalyuri had filled the role of prime
primitive. He had visited civilization and lived on the fringes
of settlement activity for a few weeks, although none of the
refinements of our society had adhered to him. Except for
the ghastly coat and trousers he wore, I thought he was still
an unsophisticated nomad. Yet that opinion was to change
in the next few hours. The Jambajimba boy and the relatives
we found with him were to make Jalyuri seem almost
detribalized.

We were able to cross two sandhills without much difficulty, fortunately finding low 'saddles' which were neither
too steep nor too deep for our laden trucks.

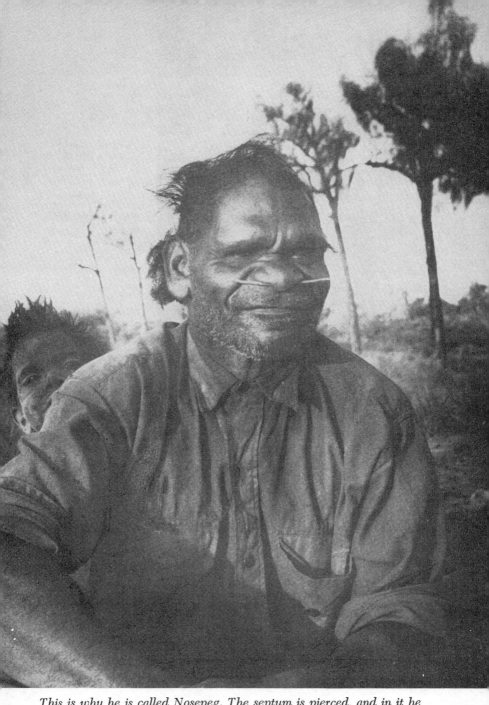

This is why he is called Nosepeg. The septum is pierced, and in it he can wear a stick or small bone.

*Primitive vanity!
Jalyuri with top-knot
of black cockatoo
feathers . . . and,
showing chest
beautifully cicatriced,
in the Stone Knife
quarry.*

Anatjari's daughter, showing excessive distension of abdomen, indicating acute malnutrition.

As we found Anatjari and his family, with inevitable lizards . . .

. . . and as he was a few days later, clothed and using a steel tyre lever to cut damper.

While driving across the valley floor to the third ridge we saw black figures against the skyline. They were on top of the ridge, camped beneath one of the small eucalypts we occasionally found on these sandy summits. As we approached — and the roar of the vehicles in the heavy going must have been a terrifying experience for them — they remained immobile, watching the progress of the first wheeled contraptions of any kind that they had seen. The urge to flee may have been upon them, but they held their ground, apparently resigned to whatever fate was in store. That moment, for them, could be compared only with the reaction of civilized people first confronted with the arrival of space ships and men or creatures from another planet. If that should ever happen to me (and as a writer I hope it does) I'll be proud if I stand as firmly.

While we were still driving I could see that the group included one man, two women and three children. The women, we learnt later, were classificatory sisters. Both were the man's wives.

As we began climbing the ridge I left the truck and walked towards the group with Nosepeg. Jeremy Long had to drive over the sand and down the other side to firm ground. That gave me the opportunity of being first to reach the aborigines and first to greet them. It was a thrilling experience, and the memory of those few moments will remain with me for the rest of my life. I was grateful to Jalyuri and Snowy, who must have prepared them for our arrival.

When twenty yards from them I waved. There was no answering gesture. They did not understand that a wave is a form of friendly greeting. They may have thought that I was wiping flies from my face.

The man stood about ten paces in front of one of his wives,

with the other a little further in the background. Except for a grass belt, he was entirely naked. The women both wore pubic cloths, but nothing else.

I approached the man with my hand extended but he did not give me his. On the contrary, he retained a firm grip on his spear and woomera, perhaps still believing that he may have to defend himself. After all, I may be a little wary of locking horns with the first Martian I meet — or whatever gesture he proposes.

When they saw his diffidence, Nosepeg and Jalyuri spoke to him. He then gave me his left wrist, but I reached for his right hand and shook it.

His face was lit by the kind of nervous smile that I cannot hope to adequately describe, but it was plain that he still didn't entirely trust me. He was seeing his first white face and, I suppose, was trying to decide whether it was as friendly as it seemed, or whether he might expect a pair of handcuffs — for he would certainly have heard the tales of cruelty from other aborigines.

I held his hand firmly for a few minutes, trying to over-come the barrier of language telepathically, and by com-municating as Helen Keller did with pressures on the fingers and palms and lips. This, combined with instructions from Nosepeg and Jalyuri, must have reassured him. He brought his left hand around and clasped me firmly on the right wrist. He then grinned broadly, disclosing a fine set of teeth as a contrast to his black skin and long black beard. He held on to my arm for several minutes while he examined me closely: he looked searchingly into my eyes and face, and the white skin on the back of my hand. While doing that he saw my wristlet watch and seemed momentarily startled by it — he would not have had the faintest idea of its purpose or how it worked. He touched my clothes gently, feeling the texture of my cheap bush shirt. Finally he spoke.

'Ahhhh!' he said.

Then there was a rapid-fire of words in his language, all of it completely unintelligible to me. I said something equally unintelligible to him in English — a greeting. The words were important, though not understood, for I felt that they put him at ease. He relaxed, released his grip on my arm, and became almost garrulous. Periodically his glance returned to my face, and when it did he repeated the only word that I think I understood.

'Ahhhh!'

It probably means in Pintubi exactly what it means in English — an expressive sigh of satisfaction. He was relieved to at last have passed the ordeal of his first meeting with a white man.

Once or twice I sensed that he was nearly overcome by emotion. I had seen thousands of aborigines, of whom he was simply one more in the physical sense, but I was a phenomenon to him, a white man coming to him across the bridges of time. As a male aboriginal, he had been trained to keep his emotions in check. He did so perfectly. Nevertheless, I was conscious of the deeper feeling beneath the black mask and wondered if, as a white man in similar circumstances, he might not have allowed tears to relieve his tensions.

From the grass string around his waist, near the circumcised and subincised penis, a dead goanna hung by its broken neck, which made me wonder if this man's welcome to us was perhaps tempered with concern that he might have to feed us. He could see that we were a party of four white men and three aborigines who would certainly impose a strain on his larder. He had never seen tinned food or flour, and could not know whether we were goanna eaters like the Pintubi or lived on the atmosphere. Did he make a quick check of his supplies, like a housewife embarrassed by unexpected guests, and estimate if there was enough to go around? Perhaps he did, for the trucks were fifty yards away; he had no opportunity to see the drums of food we carried. The poor man may even have decided to say, when mealtime came, that he felt unwell and would not eat, thereby making another goanna tail available for the visitors. Little did he know what a bacchanalia was to be provided for him, his wives and his children, with Bully Beef and Damper à la Nosepeg.

My own reaction to the meeting was predominantly of wonder and bewilderment. In the second half of the twentieth century it is a rare privilege to be the first representative of one ethnic group to be seen by a man from another. I tried, while holding his hand, to get inside this man's mind, to feel as he was feeling, to give meaning to those inexpressibly appropriate 'Ahhhhs' that he enunciated. The exercise was futile, and yet I was aware of the thrill that Stanley must have known on finding Livingstone, in spite of his nonchalant, though historic, greeting. Without much encouragement, I might have been overcome myself by emotion. That could easily have happened if we had had the facility of verbal communication — to have been able to express to each other at that moment the depth of feeling in the breasts of both of us.

This man, to me, was nothing more nor less than another human being. His skin was colourless. Having denied himself contact with the outside world, with the place and the manners that we regard as civilized, he had been unable to acquire any of the uncivilized habits of many of our contemporaries. The pattern of his behaviour, through my eyes, was neither irritating nor captivating. It might have been described as neuter. He simply was. Never having worn clothes, he was without prudery. Not having heard of lust or cheating or lying or stealing or the other crimes against society and humanity, he was amoral — a man who would have to be taught that sins existed. On learning that lesson, he would probably want to experiment, to see how they tasted or smelt or felt, and by then, of course, he would be a sinner. But I contest that this man and his family, and those we found later, were sinful on the day they were born in the manner that millions are taught today.

He might have been taken directly from this desert to the great salons of learning and, if adequate interpretation were possible, have given expert and fascinating lectures on the culture and survival of his people.

When Jeremy Long walked up the sandhill from the truck he soon confirmed, with his experience of earlier journeys and his astute questioning, that none of these people had had previous contact with Europeans.

The man's two wives were strikingly ugly, a physical fact which seemed to become more pronounced as our westerly progress continued, but one which has seldom been of apparent importance in the tribes. As far as I'm aware, ugliness has never prevented an aboriginal woman getting a husband. They are desirable assets, of course, for reasons other than as sexual partners. They are chattels who can always be traded for other goods; primarily, they are first-class food gatherers who will add to a man's larder while he is young and keep him alive when he is too old to hunt.

These two had figures which could only be described as scraggy. Their hair was knotted and dirty. A pedicure may have reduced the scale on their feet but also have inhibited the natural protection from spinifex points, thorns and stones as they walked barefooted across the desert. A manicure may have improved the appearance of their hands but would have been destroyed next day when they resumed hunting and digging for goannas. Flies crawled unheeded over their bodies and faces, and were not brushed from their eyes and noses. They were women of great stamina and endurance who could walk for hours with heavy loads of firewood on their heads. They gave birth to their children while lying on a bed of sand, attended and comforted only by each other, neither possessing any knowledge of obstetrics or hygiene or even of the cause of their own pregnancies. As with most tribal people, they would believe in immaculate conception — the implantation of a pre-existent spirit-child into the mother's womb. Physiologically, there would be no association in their minds between conception and sexual intercourse.

Utensils other than wooden coolamons and pitchis were unknown to them. In the camp there were two or three spears, a few yam sticks, a grinding stone for wild berries, a coolamon and half a dozen dead lizards — their only food.

When they hunted they armed themselves with spears. The Jambajimba boy had a spear when we found him. But I must say that I wondered why, because we did not see any kangaroos in that area and the lizards are caught by digging them out of holes. I suppose they carry spears in the hope that they will see big game, but I'm sure these weapons are seldom used to kill their food.

In the camp there were also two tame dingoes to help them in the hunt, and used as warm bodies to hug on cold winter nights. When we arrived the dingoes reverted temporarily to their wild state. They ran away and stayed in the remoteness of the sandhills until dusk. Then they crept in stealthily, wary of our presence, approaching a few yards

at a time and completing a full circuit of the camp. Finally
the smell of our food was too much for them and they came
boldly to within a few yards of us, shadowing the disposal
of our scraps for the remainder of the night. I made sure,
before rolling out my swag, that our bag of salt beef was out
of their reach on the roof of the truck. Chewed paper and
cartons, and tins that had been licked clean, testified next
morning to the wisdom of this precaution and to prodigious
canine appetites.

Nakedness must have made the lives of these people
utterly miserable in the cold weather. Alice Springs, on the
same latitude, has several weeks of near-freezing nights
every year. Little wonder, I thought, that their bodies were
scarred with burns from firesticks and campfires.

Without doubt, we had found Stone Age people, and I was
elated. But how fortunate we were to have discovered them
at all! At our dinner-camp we had been within a mile of
them, but the series of sand ridges made us unaware of their
presence, and them of ours. Except that Jalyuri and Snowy
had taken a midday walk — because fresh tracks had been
seen about three miles back — we may have driven on without making contact. That night in their camp we might have
been a thousand miles instead of one from the track we had
been following, so remote did it seem.

The man's spears were made entirely of wood. They had
no tin or iron, nor did I see any evidence of stone knives
from the deposit near Pollock Hills. There were certainly no
other weapons or implements.

Their water came from a miserable hole in the desert floor,
ten feet deep and only a yard wide. The water was grey and
full of grit, yet I imagine represented a vast lake to them.
They had never seen a running stream or water flowing from
a tap. A week later they were amazed when we showed them

a man-made tank seven feet deep, ten yards wide, and holding about five thousand gallons of clear water.

The Jambajimba boy showed us how he climbed vertically down the hole, taking precarious steps on crumbling earthern walls, much of which fell into his drink. He scooped a pint or so into a wooden coolamon and drank it in one draught.

On returning to the surface, I struck a match near the boy's face. He jumped as though the devil was after him. 'Waru! Waru!' he shouted. 'Fire! Fire!'

He looked at the burning match-stick incredulously, the greatest miracle we had produced for him yet — for fire is of vital significance in aboriginal lives. But there were others to follow. That boy and his five-year-old brother were faced with enchanting days of continuing magic as we opened tins of food and showed them worldly goods whose existence they had not imagined.

I gave them combs and mirrors and had to explain the use of both. Until I demonstrated by putting the comb through my own hair they had no idea of the purpose of these ordinary articles. The women tried to use the combs upside down. They didn't have much better success when I put them into their hands correctly, for their hair was so knotted and grime-laden that it needed washing before a comb could be used. There wasn't water enough to waste on such luxuries. The man was able to get the comb through his beard, but the women soon lost interest and in a few minutes I saw the gifts abandoned in the sand.

The mirrors were equally unsuccessful, although these people had not previously seen their own images. The man knew what his wives and children looked like but had never seen his own face. He was momentarily fascinated when I held a mirror in front of him. He examined himself search-

ingly, seeing into his own eyes for the first time. Nosepeg
had to explain that what he saw was his own image.

'Ahhhh!' he said, and studied himself again, as though he
had not been aware that his face was the face reflected
there. The women looked into the mirrors only once while
I was present. It is possible they may have regarded the
images as spirits, and that would have frightened them. On
the other hand, they may simply have disliked what they
saw — and for that I would not have blamed them. Unlike
Jugudi's two wives at Kumanadja, they were unsmiling and
seemed unhappy, especially the Number Two wife, the
younger but uglier of the two. Their faces and movements
lacked animation. They were cheerless . . . almost miserable.
The harsh life in the desert seemed to have affected their
dispositions. It was apparent that they regarded it as an
existence holding no promise of comfort or distraction. I
understood that. I would be equally miserable if told that
I had to spend the rest of my life there. But I did not understand why Jugudi's wives, in an almost identical situation,
should have been so vastly different; they had smiled constantly and been interested in everything that transpired.
Was it the water? Did it taste better or less gritty at Kumanadja than at Wudungu? Were the goannas fatter or juicier?
Was the country itself sweeter, and was that reflected in the
women's dispositions? I did not know, and had no way of
finding out. It may be, as sisters, that they were naturally
despondent. Yet two days later, at Jupiter Well, we found
four women and a man suffering from equally constant
dejection. This is remarkable only because the aborigines
are naturally happy people who laugh spontaneously, loudly,
and frequently. The slightest joke puts them in stitches and
they clamour for more. With that knowledge, I had to assume

that the hearts of these people were heavily oppressed by
their environment.

The man's name was Anatjari of the Jambajimba skin.
I developed a deep affection for him, and not only because
he contributed significantly on a later occasion to the success
of our expedition. He was not more than five feet four inches
tall, and weighed about eight and a half stones. His body
carried not a single superfluous ounce of flesh. Although on
a small scale, he was classically built with strong thighs,
tapered hips and a large chest. His heavy beard and long
hair branded him as a distinguished aboriginal. Nosepeg was
not amused by a suggestion that he should throw away his
razor and also grow a beard.

'I'm proper gentleman,' he insisted.

Anatjari's wives, Jungkaya and Mamuru, were sisters of
the Nabangadi skin. The elder took precedence, sitting
always slightly forward of the other. When they walked the
husband led, his five year old son followed, and the wives
came behind in their appropriate places. If a menial task
requiring only one woman's labour had to be done it was
always the Number Two wife who was sent. Perhaps that
is why she was even more dismal than her sister. But both
women carried the huge bundles of firewood needed to keep
them warm at night.

They camped only a few yards from us, lying in the sand
quite naked, without blankets or other covering, sharing the
warmth of the two dingoes which curled up with them —
when they weren't raiding our camp for food scraps.

All seven ate endlessly, almost as though they could not
expect to do so again after our departure. We first met them
in mid-afternoon. An hour later Nosepeg baked a damper, an
operation watched with intense interest by Anatjari and his

family. They began eating as soon as it was ready, with side-dishes of tinned meat, jam, milk, tea and sugar. From then until dark, when the women and children 'retired' to their separate camp, I saw no apparent pause in their eating. Anatjari, certainly, was never without food in his mouth. He did not eat greedily — in fact, I thought his manner of eating without a knife or fork was rather refined — but he ate constantly. Nosepeg had to make another damper. The first one, perhaps three feet in circumference, had not satisfied them. They regarded it as Christmas pudding.

A baby girl, two or three years old, clawed large lumps of damper into her mouth, alternating it with meat from a minute goanna she had personally cooked in hot ashes. She ate her way along it after using her tiny fingers to expertly remove entrails that were apparently distasteful to her. Her small half-sister sat in the dirt and kept pace with a tin of bully beef, scraping it out with her fingers, enjoying it as though she was attending her first birthday party. Next morning I examined that tin. It was licked so clean that it was shiny.

I gave them both boiled lollies, but they had no idea what to do with them until I put one in each mouth. Thus began their knowledge of sweets.

These people might well have starved in the midst of plenty if required to open the tins of meat and the packets of food we gave them. They had no implement sharp enough to open a tin, and no conception of how to get to the inside of a packet. They were prepared to eat potatoes and onions raw until told to cook them.

Like most Central Australian aborigines, Anatjari chewed a native narcotic — pituri — which had been roasted in cork-wood ash. But he had never seen or smoked a cigarette. If there was any doubt about whether or not he had previously

had contact with Europeans it vanished when I gave him
two. He put them in his mouth together. Only after patient
instruction by Nosepeg did he manage to make an untidy
job of smoking one.

He had no idea what it was when I gave him a few
shillings. Nosepeg explained that the coins were money — I
heard him use that word — but they meant nothing to this
nomad. When Nosepeg and Jalyuri establish their chain of
Hot Dingo stands and Artifact Alleys that situation will
change and money will attain the importance that it has
elsewhere. But at that moment Anatjari would not have
hesitated if offered a choice between a five pound note and
a pound of flour.

Frank Few, the American cameraman, said: 'Now you've
ruined everything. You've introduced Yankee capitalism to
this unspoilt desert. Next time we come out here this guy
will own a chain of waterholes.'

Again I wished that I could speak the Pintubi tongue and
thus be able to communicate directly with this independent
self-reliant man of the desert. I wanted to discover what
made him remain in such an inhospitable land, and to discuss
his religion, his ceremonies, and his problems. I especially
wished to hear from him his story of the privations they
suffered in moving from one waterhole to another in the hot
weather. How did naked babies manage to survive in almost
shadeless baked sand with the sun temperature above a
hundred and fifty degrees? How did women suckle infants
when malnutrition had emptied and deflated their breasts?
How often did the family sleep at night without having eaten
that day, especially when summer heat inhibited the hunter's
endurance? What was the longest period they had ever
existed without food? Who had circumcised him, and where

Her first tin of bully beef — and she loved it! This small girl suffered from yaws.

His first drinking utensil other than a wooden pitchi . . . and he didn't quite know how to use it.

Their first party . . . with slabs of damper and a 4-gallon drum of water. They thought it was Christmas.

Jeremy Long, Anatjari and family. Note girl with lizard and another behind woman's back.

The only children not malnourished were those still suckling. Flies seemed not to be noticed.

and when, and with what instrument? How many people did he know of who had perished from thirst or starvation or exhaustion?

These and dozens of other questions demanded answers but I resisted the urge to ask them, fearing that Nosepeg might be diffident about discussing matters of a personal nature. I also suspected that Nosepeg, invaluable as he was, sometimes supplied answers from his own knowledge. That would have been done in good faith, but these were questions I wanted answered by Anatjari or not at all.

Our communication was therefore limited. Nevertheless, I saw enough to form my own opinion as to the manner of life of the Pintubi nomads. Simultaneously I developed a profound respect for their intelligence, their dignity, their will to live, and the absolute authority of the men in their own 'household'.

The utter primitiveness of Anatjari and his wives can perhaps best be understood by relating it to a few of the commonplace things of European society.

None of them had seen a building of any kind, running water, soap, clothes, knives, forks, spoons, sheep, cows, horses or any animal bigger than a kangaroo. But one day in 1956 a group of Pintubi, not including Anatjari, did see the terrifying tracks of a cloven-hoofed animal crossing their tribal land from west to east. They would have run away, but among them was the Jabangadi man who had been a stockman on the Canning stockroute before returning to desert nomadism. He identified the tracks as those of a rogue bullock. Rain had recently fallen and it had been enticed hundreds of miles from its home country by surface water and the parakelia. They stalked and killed it with wooden spears after what must have been an epic chase

and an agonizing death. The intruder's tracks were soon
obliterated by the wind. Others like them were never again
seen in the desert.

Each waterhole and mountain has a name but the country
in which they live, as a whole, is known to the Pintubi as
Judjakutja. Anatjari and his family had not heard the word
'Australia'. They did not know it was the name of the biggest
island continent in the world. They did not know that they
lived on an island continent. None of them had heard of Mr
Menzies, Mr Khrushchev, President Kennedy, Mr Macmillan,
Alice Springs, the sea, or hydrogen bombs. They were
mystified when told that white men from nations across
oceans they could not comprehend had killed millions of
people in two wars. They had never seen firearms, although
Anatjari and his family, like Gunia and Wadi at Papunya and
Jugudi at Kumanadja, had been terrified by infrequent aeroplanes flying over their land. He confirmed that they, too,
had 'planted' themselves among spinifex bushes.

How could one begin to explain to these simple people
some of the wonders of civilization? Trying to describe such
magical things as television sets, moving pictures and automatic lifts and staircases would have been an impossible
task. How, then, could one make them understand the ultimate miracle of the age: astronauts orbiting the earth and
returning safely through the atmosphere in man-made cap-
sules? How could I convey to them that a motor car had
travelled at four hundred miles an hour, and an aeroplane at
three times the speed of sound? None of that was possible.
I wished, however, for the ability to tell them the simpler
story that I would write a book which would one day be
printed, and that their young relatives being taught at
Papunya and Yuendumu settlements would be able to read
it. And I wanted to tell them that the wheels that made our

slow-moving vehicles possible had their first crude counter-
parts thousands of years ago, about the time their ancestors
reached Australia from the north and north-west and in-
explicably left the lush green coastline for the dry red
interior. The wheel was as old as their Dreamtime, yet they
had never seen one. The only 'building' they knew was a
rough shelter of spinifex and mulga branches thrown around
the base of a desert oak.

Anatjari's two small daughters showed signs of malnutrition. They had distended abdomens and were also suffering
from yaws, which wasn't improved by the blanket of flies
adhering to their bodies.

Before dawn they stoked the fires against the biting cold
of the south-east trade winds and prepared for a day of rest
from hunting while they ate our food. But in a few days they
would be out in the desert again with their spears and digging sticks, hoping for kangaroos which seldom came, and
having to settle for Muddy Water Soup, Goanna Entrée, and
a dessert of wild berries.

In the firelight I could see a small girl crawling on her
hands and knees to stoke her own fire. She could not walk
properly. She put her tiny head down to blow on the coals
so that the mulga sticks would ignite and give her warmth.
She was naked and must have been very cold. But she did
not cry. There were three small children in that camp, yet
while we stayed there I did not hear one whimper. Nor was
there a single word of disapproval or a cry of dismay later in
the day when their father left them with their mothers to
fend for themselves while he joined us for the ride to Jupiter
Well. We gave them food, but that would soon be exhausted.
When that happened they must hunt to live, a necessity not
made easier for the Number One wife by the fact that one
of her wrists was bent in a semi-circle. It had been smashed

in a stick fight with another woman and allowed to mend, without splints, as best it could.

I revisited Wudungu waterhole. I sat beside it, wondering again what pleasure these people could possibly get from life. The tired hunter and his family went there to drink only as a physical need to prevent them perishing. They would not contemplate drinking for its own sake, a fact which I understood well on closer inspection of the water.

The date was August 7, 1963. Our position was 126 degrees East longitude and 22 degrees 50 minutes South latitude. The Pintubi had been there for perhaps ten thousand years, yet Anatjari did not know, geographically, where he was. Nor had he any idea of our tables of time.

If someone had explained them he would not have been interested, for one day in the desert is like any other day, one year the same as the next. The sun shone for more than three hundred days of every year. Winter cold was as inevitable as summer heat, but was mercifully briefer.

Time was measured twice a year by hot weather and cold weather, and twice a day by sunrise and sunset, but they did not know this celestial clockwork was caused by the rotation of the earth on its axis and its revolution around the sun. They did not know the earth was round. They did not know it wasn't flat. They knew, simply, that it was.

Age wearied them, but the physiological changes which greyed a man's hair and slowed his body were an unknown mystery. A Pintubi was old when his beard was white, and probably past his prime at thirty-five. We estimated that Anatjari was about that age. An average healthy white man could expect to look no older at forty-five. I found it difficult to say with any certainty whether a woman was twenty or forty. Anatjari's Number One wife appeared to me to be fifty. Her face and body were deeply lined, her eyes were wrinkled, and her hair was grey and knotted. Yet she was probably not much older than her husband.

Whatever her age, she had lived in that desert every day of her life. It had left indelible marks upon her.

The Runner of the Dunes

Inevitably, tattered shirt and trousers were produced from someone's bottomless swag for Anatjari. Whether he simply wanted to be warm or whether he had suddenly become self-conscious about his nudity I do not know, but he hastened to put them on.

Robert Benchley at his best could not have given a more amusing five minutes than the hilarity provided naturally by this primitive man in a vain endeavour to get into the garments unaided.

He had not the slightest idea how to go about it.

At one stage he had both feet inside the legs of the trousers — but from the wrong end.

Doing up and undoing the buttons was completely beyond him. In his lifetime he had been involved with no more complex mechanical process than fitting a woomera to the end of his spear shaft. Making a button go through a buttonhole, in places he could not easily see, was impossibly difficult for him, and he had to be helped. So was the reverse process of getting the buttons undone. Once or twice this proved embarrassing when Anatjari wanted to 'go along lavatory', as Nosepeg explained modestly. Even though they were rags, he was terribly proud of his first shirt and trousers, but I'm sure he wished himself naked again just then, especially in view of my ill-concealed laughter at his difficulties. On one such occasion the truck was stopped at his request. He climbed down from the load, walked a few feet from the track, and squatted on his knees before beginning to fumble with the buttons. I was forced to look elsewhere — I could not stand the suspense. But I made one discovery, later substantiated: these Pintubi men sit to urinate.

In this humourless country we had a few laughs and they were so much funnier because they were frequently compounded with pathos, as in the case of Anatjari and his buttons. Charlie Chaplin's admirers will remember that it was this element which lifted his clowning into the class of genius. He was such a pathetic figure that his audience wept while overcome with hysterical laughter. No wonder I was fascinated by Anatjari, while despising myself for observing him so rudely and so closely.

But if we had our laughs we gave some, too. Anatjari, his five-year-old son, Wili, and the fourteen-year-old Jambajimba boy, Nim-Nim, came with us in the trucks for the forty mile ride to Jupiter Well, about two hundred miles west of the Northern Territory border and five hundred and forty miles from Alice Springs. Our nearest civilization at that point was Carnegie cattle station, four hundred and seventy miles south-west, and Papunya settlement, three hundred and eighty miles to the east. Whichever way we travelled, it was too far to walk; both vehicles had been boiling and suffering from pre-ignition, which sounded like indigestion, and I hoped they would be equal to the long haul home. As it happened, this mechanical dyspepsia disappeared when we turned their faces into the easterly winds.

Anatjari and the two boys were delighted, if a little fearful, with their first ride in motor trucks. It must have seemed strange to them to see the ground and trees flashing by at twice walking speed, which was as much as we could manage

over long stretches of heavy sand. They must have felt that
the jet age had arrived when we occasionally touched thirty
or forty miles an hour.

Jupiter Well stood in an unusually dense grove of desert
oaks and ti-trees. The area had previously been visited by
surveyors from the Division of National Mapping, Department of National Development, and by Len Beadell and his
partners in the Gun Barrell Road Construction Company.
They dug and timbered the well and there we found the
first supply of water adequate for bathing that we had seen
in more than three hundred miles. My spirit was lifted
simply by being near so much water — a hole ten feet deep
and five feet wide, with a hinged lid on top to prevent silting
and a rope for attaching to buckets so that it could be drawn
efficiently. Such luxury! Such modernity! But such water!
It tasted like a mixture of cough medicine and the Pacific
Ocean. Our tanks were almost empty, however, and we were
obliged to use it for cooking and drinking.

But let me not be too disparaging. To the desert men it
was an excellent supply. And to us it meant a long overdue
bath, the first since leaving Haasts Bluff. We stripped and
bathed in a sawn-off drum in water less than knee-deep,
using salt-water soap for lathering. This was the *quid pro quo*
for my laughs at the expense of the Pintubi.

The Jambajimba boy, who had become even more of a
shadow, stood and watched us open-mouthed, highly amused
by our naked white flesh but, if I read his face correctly, also
a little aghast that good water should be wasted so prodi-
gally. Apart from this squandering of what was, to him,
exclusively a life-giving fluid, he was fascinated by the
mechanics of bathing, by the soaping, the lathering, the
rinsing and, I've no doubt, by the ecstatic sighs and the
grampus-like blowing that accompanied our ablutions.

He had never taken a bath in his life. Nor had any of his ancestors. In the rainy weather they may have been wet occasionally, but that would have been regarded as a discomfort rather than a cleansing process. These people felt extremely fortunate if they had enough water to drink. To waste it as we did must have been a shock to his system. Nevertheless, he was highly amused at the sight of us washing and emerging even several shades whiter of skin than he believed us to be. I had been congratulating myself on an excellent sun-tan, but adequate water showed me what an illusion that was. It all came off in the wash. We had eaten and slept at dirt-level for more than a week. The dirt is redbrown, and that was the colour of our bodies. This effect was not so noticeable with the aborigines, whose black skins tended to turn grey rather than brown under the heavy coating of dust. Having changed my colour, I felt as a chameleon must feel when it enters a new environment. And, ah, the luxury of clean clothes! My socks, my shirt and singlet were impregnated with red which was simply part of the desert. I washed them under these primitive conditions and succeeded only in converting the dust to dye. But at least in my fresh apparel I must have been a little less objectionable to my neighbours.

One of the most impressive episodes of our trip so far occurred that day, with Anatjari as the star.

At Jupiter Well we found the tracks of seven or eight aborigines and a warm campfire which indicated it had been very recently abandoned. On a sand ridge beneath big desert oaks (which are said to indicate shallow sub-artesian water) I saw the remains of a camp that reminded me of a city doss-house or an overcrowded dormitory.

In a land where millions of acres wasted, a 'bed' had been

scooped from the sand. The indentations of bodies remained, and the entire area was just seven bodies wide with room for fires between each person. Children and babies would somehow have found sleeping room there, too. Such 'togetherness' was undoubtedly dictated by the primary need to give maximum protection during cold desert nights, but I wondered if that could not have been as satisfactorily achieved with bigger individual fires a few yards distant from each other. The desert oaks provided ample firewood, and husbands and wives would thus have acquired a little privacy. At no time did I find, however, that privacy was either sought or valued. A man lay in the dirt at night with two or three wives and their children. Sexual intercourse probably occurred at times between a husband and one wife in full view of the others. Apparently that did not worry them, for opportunities to arrange it otherwise were readily available.

When I say that 'we' found the tracks of other aborigines I mean, of course, that they were found by Nosepeg, Jalyuri, Anatjari and Snowy. Try as I might, I always saw tracks of any kind after they saw them. They could not read or write a word or sign their names, but the ground was an open book. As in other places, Nosepeg told us not only that aborigines had been in the camp the day before, but also their names. This astonished me when one man, Jugudi, was identified by his tracks at Kumanadja rockhole. It seemed almost unbelievable that after a further three hundred miles of desert travelling they could identify the tracks of an entire group of people.

'How do you know?' I asked Nosepeg. I pointed to a footprint and asked him to show me what made him so sure that it belonged to a particular person. I wanted to be shown if one person had hammer toes and another, perhaps, was pigeon-toed.

Nosepeg could not do that. 'We just know 'im — like reading book,' he said.

Well, I suppose there is logic in that. After all, I'd be hard-pressed to explain why I know that the letter 'A' is the letter 'A', except by its shape and size. I just 'know 'im'.

Anatjari's stardom was directly linked with our attempt to find the people who made these tracks. That it was a successful attempt, and culminated in our meeting with eleven more remarkable people, was due entirely to him.

We drove another fifteen miles along our westerly track and then tried pushing south towards a waterhole these men knew about. But our way was barred by treacherous sandhills too high for the vehicles to cross.

The tracks of the people we were now looking for led through them, along an unmarked desert pad that was easily negotiated by men on foot but was impassable, except at too great a risk, even for four-wheel-drive trucks.

We climbed a rocky escarpment and from there Nosepeg pointed out a feature on the horizon, perhaps another fifteen miles away, and told us that the Pintubi who had so recently been at Jupiter Well were probably camped there.

'Good water there,' he said. 'Might be people there, I reckon. But too much sand. No good for truck.' And if Nosepeg said the sand was too deep his word could be taken for granted, for he had an inflated faith in the abilities of wheeled vehicles.

The question, then, was how to make contact. The answer was easy: on foot. But it wouldn't be easy for the owner of the feet.

I would have volunteered to go except that it was too far

and I didn't know the way. Nor am I fond of walking in the desert where the view is so monotonous.

It was suggested to Jalyuri that he might walk to that distant point and ask the people whose tracks he had helped identify to come in to us.

But Jalyuri was tired. He had been sitting in a truck for a week, and eating and sleeping more than usual. That takes it out of a man. The idea that he should walk thirty miles or so to find others of his kind (for he would have to walk back, too) did not appeal to him. He laughed non-committally and said a few words in the dialect, unintelligible to me, the import of which could have been, 'Not bloody likely'.

Nosepeg turned to us and said disgustedly, 'Ah, he's too lazy!'

Although a man of considerable influence, Nosepeg did not have the authority to compel him to go. Among the tribesmen there are very few bosses; they are independent men who will not take orders from others . . . especially orders involving hardship and physical exercise of the type now being proposed.

'Why don't you go, Nosepeg?' I asked.

'Can't. I'm not too lazy meself, but my legs are little-bit-lazy,' he said. 'They don't want to go over too many sand hills.'

Anatjari was our man.

He knew the country as well as it knew him. Throughout his life he had been in touch with it with his bare feet, sensitive feet co-ordinating splendidly with his hunter's eyes in spite of calloused and crusty soles. They had to be like ironstone to resist the twin tortures of spiked spinifex and boiling sand. A protective sheath of scale covered the insteps and ankles. His calves and thighs were finely honed, having carried him on the daily hunt . . . twenty? thirty? forty miles?

. . . since he was old enough to wield a spear. Jalyuri knew the country, too, as he had demonstrated in the sandhills near Mamu, but Anatjari was at home here, having been hunting only fifty miles away when we found him. He and his wives and children would have lived on these waterholes before moving east. The people we wanted to find were his next-door neighbours. He would know where to go to knock on their door.

When the proposition was put to him by Nosepeg, at Jeremy Long's request, Anatjari did not hesitate. The serried hills, stark and forbidding, did not deter him, for that was the environment in which he had grown to manhood. Only two days earlier he met white men for the first time; he found them friendly and broke damper with them; he opened their miraculous tins and packets of food; he watched his children drinking milk which also came from tins; he rode on one of their vehicles, speeding through his domain so that . . . and this was another 'first' for him . . . the wind whistled in his ears. He now seemed keen to carry the word to others: 'Come on in. Get your share of damper and tinned meat. See the strange men who wear clothes. See the vehicles which take the walking out of travel.' Or words to that effect.

He climbed down from the back of the truck and was instantly ready to go. He did not need to pack a bag. There were no last minute messages to send. Farewells were unnecessary. Normally he would not take a cut-lunch, but live on the goannas he caught on the way. However, this was to be a rather special occasion calling for unorthodox preparations.

Long gave him rations — tea, sugar and raisins — which he tied in a cloth around his neck. He carried his own piece of damper, cigarettes, and matches — white man's 'waru' — in a billycan. Before leaving he drank perhaps half a gallon of water — enough to sustain him for a long time, because his next drink must come from the niggardly desert.

I thought it was a pity that Anatjari wore unaccustomed clothes. I would have preferred to watch him walking across those dunes as he always had, wearing nothing more than the grass belt around his waist as a goanna-carrier. Shirt and trousers would inhibit his movement, and certainly his appearance, but we had little chance of taking them from him for impractical aesthetic reasons. At least he would be warmer at night than customarily, and he might soon discover that the pockets could be used as hold-alls — a convenience which, in view of the cigarettes and matches in the billycan, he had apparently overlooked.

Anatjari told his five-year-old son and fourteen-year-old tribal brother, the Jambajimba boy, to stay with Jalyuri. Then, without another word, he set off across the valley to the first sandhill, walking quickly and erectly.

He did not once look back towards us, but I did see him turn his head to take the time on his watch . . . the sun's height above the horizon.

I thought I heard him say to himself, but it may only have been the wind . . . 'It's late!' . . . With that, near the base of the sandhill, he broke into a run and went up it in a few seconds, leaving a wake of red dust at his feet.

I cheered him silently. He was going into country where I would surely have soon been lost and perished. Darkness would overtake him long before he reached the waterhole. He had no blanket.

I guessed he would walk for a while in the moonlight, and fall down to sleep when fatigued, first lighting a fire to combat the chill winds.

He was a small man in an immense desert, five-feet-four

in fifty million acres. Yet as he ran and walked up that sand-hill he became, to me, a man of giant stature. I knew then that he was really bigger than the desert, for he had known it all his life. He knew its secrets and had learned to live with it; he knew its moods, its dangerous tantrums, and its miniature storehouses of food and reservoirs of water.

Out of sight of our vehicles, I would have regarded myself as being in mortal peril. Anatjari was simply at home.

Jeremy Long arranged with Anatjari that he should put up a smoke signal to guide us towards him on his return trip next day.

I rolled out my swag that night hoping that when we saw the smoke and reached it — if we could get through — we would see not only our runner of the dunes but the other horde who lived as he did . . . west of Alice Springs, east of the Canning stockroute, north-east of Wiluna, south-west of Hall's Creek . . . in the devil country where no intelligent white man and few detribalized aborigines could hope to survive.

At Kumanadja rockhole Jugudi the Jagamara impressed me deeply with his hunting prowess, his control over the desert. Two hundred miles further west Anatjari the Jambajimba took first place in my esteem.

At Jupiter Well my prize-list was up for review again, but Anatjari held his place against competitors he brought with him . . . people who, for sheer primitiveness, were as far ahead of him as he had been of the Jagamara.

The south-east trade winds were stronger and colder than usual in the piccaninny dawn. On the fringes of the desert where habitation is, they are known as The Lazy Winds — they're too lazy to blow around you; they go straight through. I had a sleeping bag and three blankets, but I was still not warm and reached down to pull the canvas swag cover around me.

As I did so I remembered that Anatjari was lying out in the sandhills somewhere, without a blanket at all, protected only by a clump of spinifex and a fire. Even so, I thought, he would be warmer than usual, for now he had a shirt and trousers.

Nosepeg and Jalyuri must have been thinking about him, too. Their incessant talk, almost conspiratorial in its intensity, began before dawn. When the rest of the campers were awake — and that wasn't long delayed with such an efficient alarm clock as the Pintubi language — I asked Nosepeg what he thought of the chances that Anatjari had made contact with his tribesmen.

Nosepeg, gay as ever, said: 'He got 'im all right. Big mob, too. They're camped just out there now — not far . . . little-bit-long-way might-be.'

'How do you know that? How can you possibly know that?' I demanded. Although I detected good-natured bantering in his voice there were also overtones of the mock-seriousness aborigines often use when predicting an event. I knew from twenty years of personal contact that in such circumstances they had an uncanny habit of being right.

Nosepeg laughed it off again. 'I sent him a big dreaming,' he said, 'and that Jambajimba sent me one, too.'

When the sun had cleared the first ridge I walked half a mile through the sandhills, away from the desert oaks limiting our horizon, and climbed to a vantage point to make my own observations — to sneak a glance at the southern sky while Nosepeg and Jalyuri weren't watching. I was rewarded by a view of the other side of the sandhills, and nothing more.

No smoke was visible, so I dismissed Nosepeg's dream as

part of his unquenchable good fun. Long decided to give
Anatjari until midday to get back. If he had not then returned
we would drive out along the track and send up our own
smoke.

Promptly at noon, almost as though he knew of this
arrangement, Anatjari walked in through the timber, moving
appreciably slower than when I had seen him hastening up
a sandhill yesterday to find a trail and people.

Now his pace was governed by that of the old man beside
him . . . a lone naked nomad, short and bearded, who came
diffidently forward with him.

Unlike Anatjari when we first met him, this man did not
speak at all. I think he was too hungry, too thirsty, and too
tired.

He went down on his knees, with Nosepeg beside him, and
for five minutes did not utter one syllable, submitting
patiently to be photographed while not having the slightest
idea what was happening. He sat back on his heels and urin-
ated in the sand, involuntarily it seemed, without apparently
knowing or caring that he was doing so.

In his right hand he carried a wooden spear. It was
polished and clean, without bloodstains that would betray
that it had been recently used to kill substantial game.

In his left hand he hugged his only food — two fungoid
truffles and four or five spiked Mountain Devils, also known
as Thorny Devils and Thorny Lizards. When they move,
which isn't often, their slow uncertain movements resemble
a mechanical toy.

The Mountain Devil has been described as 'nine inches of
oddity in lizard form'. I agree that it is odd but I have not
yet seen one nine inches long. Those that this man carried
averaged about six inches. They are quaint animals, fasting
for several days but then eating about one thousand black

ants, their staple food, at one meal. As far as I can discover, they have never been seen to drink. The Devil's skin is hygroscopic, allowing it to absorb moisture from the atmosphere. In the Gibson Desert, that seemed to me to be a sensible way to live. I have known men to carry Devils in pockets and inside their shirts. The Pintubi, however, carried them for the sole reason that they were his only food. It had never occurred to me that they might be edible to human beings, but for this man they were certainly so. Emergency rations, perhaps, but undoubtedly 'tucker'.

He drank a full billycan of water without pausing for breath, until his belly was full and distended more than it already was by malnutrition. Nosepeg gave him a piece of his culinary art — a huge lump of damper, doughy and spongy and coated with dirt. This was the first time he had seen food of any kind made with flour — in fact, he did not know it was flour — but he must have liked it because he ate without pause for three hours. At three o'clock he made it a two-course meal by eating the Mountain Devils he cooked by burying them in hot ashes.

His name was Yaliti of the Jangala skin. He was grey-haired, grey-bearded, and not more than five feet three inches tall. I estimated his weight as seven and a half stones and his age as sixty five. His wrinkled skin was mottled with pink scar tissue, the result of firestick burns and of rolling into his campfire at night. His feet looked like the scaly body of a mullet. He had never worn a stitch of clothing in his life and now his only adornment was a grass string tied around his hair. I detected no trace of self-consciousness about his nudity; as with Anatjari, it was his natural state. Unlike other Pintubi males, he did not bother with a string around his waist as a carry-all for goannas and other game. I wondered if it was made unnecessary by their very paucity . . . was he

always so hungry that whatever food he found was eaten
instantly?

As he squatted before me, urinating again in the sand
while continuing to eat, I felt that he was by far the most
primitive man we had seen. If he had crawled rather than
walked . . . if he carried a club and had a receding forehead
like the Neanderthals I would not have been surprised.
Jugudi the Jagamara and Anatjari the Jambajimba were
civilized by comparison. Anatjari, at least, had expressed
himself with eloquent 'Ahhhhs' when we met. He had reacted
spontaneously to his first meeting with white men. Yaliti did
not speak; he seemed to be reserving all his energy for eating.
He regarded me through half-closed eyes, which made me
think he was wide awake; but they were expressionless,
lacking visible emotion. His narrowed gaze was concentrated on my face, but I could read there none of the strong
reactions which had beset Anatjari in similar circumstances.
He was a stoic who suffered but showed it not; a lifetime of
being tortured by nature had extinguished his fire; his eyes
were burnt holes with the glow absent.

I was frustrated more than ever by my inability to talk
directly with him. It had seemed important to talk to Anatjari
in his own tongue, but with this man! — it was vital that
someone should do so before his remarkable story of survival
vanished forever. I wanted to know about the privations his
tribesmen and women had withstood, to take him back
through his earliest memories and have him tell me the complete story of his existence for as long as it had been going
on. That was not possible through an interpreter, and I had
to be satisfied with the recitation of rather repetitious detail.
I did learn that his father had seen the Hon. David Carnegie
on his journey of exploration in 1896. The story of that meeting, certain to have been passed on orally to Yaliti, would

alone have been a fascinating tale. I was not concerned that
I couldn't tell him about the outside world, the world in
which he lived but hadn't visited. He was too old to understand, to appreciate, or even to believe what he was told.
He was a rare man who would probably end his days without
learning of such simple magic as water flowing from taps.
He was born and he would die in the Gibson Desert, believing it to be the hub of his universe. It was therefore a great
disappointment to me that I was unable to share his
experiences.

I showed Yaliti my wristlet watch and pointed to the sun,
the time-piece that he used, but it meant nothing to him.
If I had asked Nosepeg to explain that it was a refrigerator
or a waffle-iron Yaliti would not have been wiser.

Like Anatjari, he knew nothing of the world wars or the
name — Australia — of the country he lived in.

The septum of his nose was pierced in Pintubi tribal
fashion but he was not wearing a bone through it. Perhaps,
like Nosepeg, he found it awkward when turning over in bed.

Never in his life had he made fire with a safety match.
One of the few flickers of astonishment I saw in his eyes
occurred when I struck a match in front of him. Having
taken little interest in my watch, my pen, my clothes or other
bits of magic, he was finally impressed by a match — for fire
was to him, more than to me, one of his four fundamental
elements.

And he went on eating . . . and eating.

He drank his first milky tea from a billycan which only a
day earlier had contained motor oil. I'm not sure whether it
was the oil or the tea he liked, but I thought he would drink
forever.

Nosepeg gave Yaliti his first lesson in the proprieties of
eating civilized food by showing him how to dunk a piece of

crusty damper in tea before eating it. Yaliti attempted to emulate him by wanting to dunk the entire damper in tea. He was defeated only because it wouldn't fit into the billy-can.

Flies were there in millions, adhering to everything and everybody, breeding mysteriously in a sterile area apparently containing none of the refuse they thrive on.

Anatjari, our man from Marathon, was hungry and thirsty, too. He was now at ease in our camp and did not have to be invited to eat. He kept pace with Yaliti in what could well have been billed, in the right environment, as The Great Damper Eating Contest. Damon Runyon's gargantuan pie-eaters, Miss Violette Shumberger, Mr Nicely-Nicely Jones and Mr Joel Duffle, would assuredly have taken stock before entering into professional competition against either of them. In one hilarious event, Miss Shumberger and Mr Duffle ate two quarts of ripe olives, twelve bunches of celery, four pounds of shelled nuts, twelve dozen cherrystone clams, two gallons of pepper-pot soup, two five-pound striped bass (the heads and tails not to count), a twenty-two pound roast turkey, twelve pounds of mashed potatoes with brown gravy, two dozen ears of corn on the cob, two quarts of lima beans, twelve bunches of asparagus cooked in butter, ten pounds of stewed peas, and six pounds of mixed green salad. Runyon fans will remember that the competition was won on a T.K.O. by Miss Shumberger when Joel Duffle couldn't leave his corner for the start of the final round — a pumpkin pie two feet across and three inches deep. Later Miss Shumberger admitted that her appetite wasn't normal because an hour before the contest she had eaten her regular dinner of pigs' knuckles and sauerkraut. I felt that this was a mistake she could not have afforded if her opponent had been either Anatjari or Yaliti.

Anatjari showed how much at home he was by asking
Nosepeg to pass the jam. He used his hand as a spoon,
scooping out a sufficient portion of Mr Gordon Edgell's dark
plum and affixing it with his palm to his piece of damper.

But ah! . . . now his hand was greasy with jam, and he
evidently did not like the sticky feeling. This was a new
experience for him, and a fascinating little study for me. He
looked accusingly at his hand and wondered what to do with
it. He had not yet been taught to lick his fingers or wipe
them on the inside of his pockets or on his trousers. Normally
he would have wiped greasy fingers through his hair, the
built-in dish-cloth carried by every aboriginal. But jam was
different; he had never had occasion to wipe that on his hair.
He hit upon a brilliant alternative. His five-year-old son was
sitting beside him, so he used his face and hair instead,
wiping his hand fondly over the lad's nose, eyes, forehead
and hair. The boy licked off as much as he could reach with
his tongue and left the rest for the flies, which didn't take
long to find it.

When Yaliti came in to us with Anatjari we were told that
four women and six children were following. That meant
some of the children would be walking. The pace of the
group would be governed by the slowest child.

One of the women was Mani Nungarai, the old man's wife.
The three others were their daughters Lubira, Payungu and
Kayukayu, all of the Nambajimba skin. Lubira had three
children, one a baby only a few months old. Payungu's son,
aged about four, was so badly infected with yaws that he
crawled but could not stand upright to walk. Kayukayu had
one son. The sixth child, a three year old girl, was these
women's sister and their children's aunt, although some of
them were older. She was Yaliti's and Mani's daughter. The

three younger women were all wives of a man of the Jaban-gadi skin who had gone off hunting with a separate group, including their teen-age brother.

The ten women and children arrived in duck formation, walking towards us through the bush in Indian file, coming in for their first sight of . . . they knew not what. As befitted her position, Mani led; her daughters followed, in the order appropriate to their status as wives.

I was struck forcefully by their dismal aspect and their obvious need of medical aid. Apart from yaws in several of the children, they all appeared to be suffering from advanced malnutrition. The abdomens of two or three of the older children were so distended from lack of vitamins that they seemed almost to be fat. However, one needed only to glance at their frail thighs, no bigger than my forearm, and their stick-like upper-arms to be aware that these people knew starvation.

I thought I had seen aborigines with insufficient to eat when we met Jugudi the Jagamara and Anatjari the Jamba-jimba in their natural environment. But Yaliti the Jangala and his horde were in infinitely worse condition. Jeremy Long said that in five years of patrolling the area he had not seen poorer people.

I'm sure the six years of drought the area has known has affected them seriously. I was told by Pintubi at Papunya and Yuendumu that mice and rats formed part of their regular diet, yet I did not see one mouse or one rat in the time we were in the desert. Nor did I see a snake, although they may have been hibernating. The fact is that their meat supply seemed inadequate to sustain them, a theory tested with startling results by a patrol in 1960 to Lake Mackay and the Kintore Ranges led by the Chief Welfare Officer, E. C. Evans. On that occasion Evans arranged for three youths aged fifteen to seventeen years to spend all of one day hunting for natural game. They were promised that they would be rewarded if they brought back their entire catch. The result was one small spinifex snake about three feet long, one lizard seven inches long, and one small goanna. The total meat available would not have sustained those three healthy young men, particularly after an exhausting hunt over sandhills and through spinifex.

The Evans report ended significantly: 'This test, while not necessarily conclusive, was nevertheless carried out in country around Kunjarri rockhole which is claimed by the people to be better 'tucker country' than that further west. In addition, in normal circumstances, these men would have been required to share their trophies of the hunt with other relatives.'

The knowledge of this 'test' hunt, and Yaliti's miserable handful of truffles and of Mountain Devils, confirmed beyond doubt the almost unbelievable poverty the Pintubi had overcome not only for generations but for millennia. I was not in the least surprised by the malnutrition produced by conditions which amounted almost to famine. I was surprised, however, that around Jupiter Well there should not have been evidence of bigger game — of kangaroos or euros. Adequate shelter was available. They don't need much water (scientific tests have shown they extract sufficient moisture from their food) so the lid on the well should not have affected them.

By European standards, and even by the standards of other aborigines, Yaliti's women and children were all very dirty. They were born in the dirt, they lived in the dirt, they slept in the dirt, and they died in the dirt. Their beds this night and every other night of their lives were on the ground, with the sand for a mattress. When you've never known

Yaliti with a few Mountain Devils. These and two truffles were the only food he had when brought in.

Yaliti's wife, Mani, is tired. So she sleeps as she always has . . . in the dirt, watched by her family.

cleanliness, when washing would be sinful waste of water that might sustain life, dirt ceases to be dirty.

It is simply a coating for the skin, and enough of it might even act as a garment.

All these people were exactly as their ancestors must have appeared to Giles, Warburton and Carnegie during their great journeys of exploration through Central Australia last century; they were exactly as distant relatives from other tribes must have appeared to James Cook, William Dampier and the early navigators who first set foot on Australian soil and paved the way for decimation which almost accomplished the extinction of the indigenous people. The estimated aboriginal population of three hundred thousand when Governor Phillip arrived was reduced to forty-six thousand before government intervention arrested the trend towards their total disappearance. In the sanctuaries built on the foundations of a belatedly stirring national conscience, they are at last beginning to increase, reversing the subtraction sums that have been the sad lot of statisticians since the first tribal country and the first tribal waters were alienated nearly two hundred years ago.

The Pintubi disappeared into the Gibson Desert and remained there, unknown and unwanted, exactly as they were on the day of entry, for uncounted centuries. In that time they did not acquire one implement made of anything but wood or stone. Unlike other primitive peoples, they made no attempt to weave fur or fibre or to use the hides of the animals they killed to protect them from cold.

When Yaliti's wife, his daughters, his child and his grandchildren came in through the scrub none wore more than a pubic cloth. The cloth itself must have been traded from other aborigines living nearer to civilization. One of the women and all the children were entirely naked. Not one of them carried even the simplest form of grass dillybag.

They were spiritless, forlorn people, with the suffering of a century in each of their faces. Like Yaliti himself, they did not react in the slightest degree to their first sight of white faces. They seemed neither afraid nor unafraid; perhaps they knew instinctively that whatever changes came to their lives as a result of this contact their lot could not be worsened.

Nosepeg tried to impress me with his yardstick of their primitiveness. 'These people have never seen motor-car before this time,' he said.

Well, there were many other things they hadn't seen, too, but the truth of his statement was underlined when Jeremy Long started one of the vehicles and drove it to the well. They had been sitting down, concentrating on eating damper and more damper. But when the engine started and the horrifying contraption moved they got to their feet at once. I thought for a moment that they were intending to run away. They may have thought of doing so, but Nosepeg reassured them and they settled down.

The women spent the remainder of that day sitting in a group twenty yards from the men, segregated in tribal fashion by sex. They did not speak to the men unless addressed and when that happened it was generally an order — perhaps to fetch water or firewood, which they carried in drums and bundles on their heads. Drums? Our drums, of course. It did not take them long to find a use for their first domestic utensils — empty flour drums which Payungu and Kayukayu took to the well and filled with water.

Kayukayu, who had one infant daughter, appeared to be not more than fifteen years old. She may have been younger, for aborigines notoriously appear older than they are. I thought she was pregnant, but that was a mistake I made with the other women, too. Their swollen bellies probably carried nothing more than the excess fluids in their bodies caused by lack of vitamins. As their mothers squatted, the children suckled by sitting in front of them or, if they were too young to sit up, by lying across the women's knees.

I was struck by the thought that suckling babies were better fed than any of the Pintubi people, in spite of the difficulty of the mothers in making sufficient milk on their own meagre diet. Only after the infants were weaned did the signs of malnutrition become apparent.

During lunch Nosepeg and Jalyuri ate their food quickly, impatient of the delay and interruption to spear-making. This industry was now operating almost on shift-work, like a Krupp factory in wartime. Yaliti and Anatjari, however, had no thought for anything but their desire to eat damper. Between lunch and sundown they did not have a break of more than one hour. Lunch became dinner half way through the afternoon. After his few days on the fringes of civilization, Anatjari had already learned a few tricks of the white man's trades; he proved it by using the sharp end of a steel tyre lever to cut through a damper.

Our camp at Jupiter Well now included twenty-one people, only four of whom were white. Nosepeg's dream of 'a big mob' had come true. But he wasn't the only dreamer.

We had arrived at Jupiter Well (sardonically named after Jupiter Pluvius) on a Wednesday. On the Monday night, according to the story he later told Nosepeg, Yaliti had dreamed that a strange apparatus would arrive next day. They would all be terrified. The tracks of Len Beadell's road grader were still visible nearby, and they may have been on his mind when he drifted into sleep . . . to awaken in a cold sweat, fearing that whatever caused the tracks would soon be chasing them.

Yaliti had rounded up his horde at dawn, and that day put twenty miles of sandhills between them and the unknown monster. We arrived next day to find his campfires still warm. Anatjari therefore had a long walk to explain to the old man that the apparitions of his dream had come on schedule . . . but also to say that they were marvellous fun to ride in . . . that they were motor vehicles with wheels which miraculously turned when something under the lid made a noise. He would also say that these vehicles carried big quantities of flour, tea and sugar. He would have damper and raisins, tea and sugar to prove it.

Yaliti, his women and children were in such poor physical shape that Anatjari would not have to be very persuasive to convince the old man of the wisdom of joining him in the trek back to the well. Nevertheless, with the knowledge of his dream, I felt sure that if we had attempted to reach him across the sandhills in vehicles which roared and sent up spumes of red dust, he would have disappeared beyond recall into the deeper bush. He may have run for his life, and taken the horde with him, if he had remained at the well and heard the high-revving trucks approaching from several miles away. It was fortuitous, therefore, that he had his dream and went away because, paradoxically, we may not have found him otherwise.

I was sometimes impatient with Jeremy Long's boundless patience, his placidity and his thoroughness. I thought he was too slow to anger, especially when aboriginal children who had never washed climbed all over our trucks and put their feet in our food-boxes. But it was his patience and his understanding of the Pintubi and their country that made possible our contact with these people, and I thanked him silently for the important discovery of Yaliti, which he organized.

Between Long and Nosepeg I detected a deep bond of affection and mutual respect. Long allowed him freedom of action which was unique in my experience of the relationship between white master and aboriginal servant. He was the official leader of the expedition — but it was often Nosepeg who led. He suggested where we should go, and when, and Long's confidence in him was such that his advice was generally accepted. They seemed to be thoroughly attuned to the needs of the patrol. Without this happy concord we may have travelled a thousand miles through the desert without seeing one Pintubi nomad. Nosepeg called him Jerry, Jerry Long, Mister Long, Mister Jerry and Mister Jerry Long. He is a gambling man who was spreading his bets. I'm sure he felt that by going through all the permutations of names he would be on a winner some of the time.

I doubt if it is possible that more secluded people than Yaliti and his horde exist anywhere in the world today. The Bushmen of the Kalahari, the western Amazonians, the Outer Mongolians, and the Kukukukus of New Guinea may all have had little contact with the world they live in, yet I wonder how many of them have never seen people of any race other than their own?

As I have shown, both Yaliti and Anatjari were short men. This was also true of most of the Pintubi I met at Papunya and Yuendumu, although there were exceptions. Eventually I formed the opinion, though not finally convinced of its accuracy, that the severe climate and sparse food may well have affected their stature over the centuries. The Bushmen and the Snake Indians of South America who live in comparatively inhospitable regions of the globe, are also small

men. So are the Eskimos, and even the Frenchmen who are
natives of the Auvergne in France, where the soil is
notoriously poor.

But it is probably unsafe to assume that climate and food
are the only factors controlling stature. They undoubtedly
have some effect, but historical reasons may also play a part.
Who is to deny, for instance, that the Pintubi tribesmen are
descendants of the weakest of all the aboriginal people who
originally migrated to Australia from where . . . India and
Ceylon? Was it white settlement, after all, that forced them
further back, and further yet, from the good soil and the
running water into country which they could make their
own . . . only because others did not want it? Could it not be,
as the weak and the meek, that they were pushed back by
the stronger tribes of their own race?

Whatever the reasons . . . there they were, with never more
water than the bare minumum necessary to sustain life,
seldom enough food, but with too much winter cold and too
much summer heat. Yet they lived on the food they hunted
and caught, much of it by women who were either bearing
or rearing children. A few, like Anatjari and Jugudi, even
seemed happy. Anatjari didn't miss the soft life because he
had never known it, but I wondered whether, having
acquired the taste for flour and tea, he wouldn't soon follow
the tribesmen who had already forsaken the desert for
Papunya and Yuendumu settlements. If he walked, his
journey of more than three hundred miles could only be
undertaken after rain. That might mean travelling in the
hottest weather; nevertheless, I think that one day, soon, he
will go.

For Yaliti it is a different story. He is old and tired. He
could not make the trip on foot, especially with all the small
children in his horde, none of them robust. Their legs and

arms are like match-sticks, their bellies like balloons. Their backs are scarred by campfire coals and their chests by fire-sticks. They need urgent medical attention.

The desert will be a poorer place without them — if that is possible — but it would be inhumane to allow human beings to continue living as they are, on the verge of starvation.

The old people will acquire bad habits when they fall among the opiates of society without immunity to them. Men with more than one wife may soon have to fight to retain their polygamous state, for aboriginal women are fewer than the young unmarried men — the have-nots of the tribes. But they are risks that will have to be faced. We live in the second half of the twentieth century . . . much too late in the Space Age for Stone Age people.

I am a reporter. My job is to tell the story of how anonymous Australians are living and dying. I do not want to suggest what the government's policy might be in regard to the aborigines. But I do want to say that when human beings starve, when human beings perish, when human beings have neither covering to keep them warm nor water enough to drink, they should be helped.

That may best be achieved, at least for the aged, with ration depots on the fringes of their own hunting country. It may be better to take them all into Papunya or Yuendumu.

Whatever it is, their almost unbelievable hardships must be relieved.

Nosepeg agrees, and he is an authority on most matters.

'We want to bring all these people out of here. Too much lonely. Not enough tucker. Not enough water,' he said.

Yaliti Says Goodbye

Yaliti's women and children were not in the least upset because they had to spend two nights only twenty yards from 'civilization' — the camp of white men.

There were plenty of 'pickings' to be had — the perquisites which, in more sophisticated circles, would be referred to as 'fringe benefits'. Perhaps the phrase was appropriate to them, too — they camped on the fringe of the glow from Frank Few's portable power lines.

The 'pickings' were just that . . . great hunks of damper they took to bed with them. I suppose they stopped eating while asleep, but I was reminded strongly of ruminants; they were chewing when I last saw them at night, and they were still chewing at dawn.

The women built a windbreak of bushes, scooped a communal bed in the sand, lit fires between each person — and one or two at their feet as well — and waited for Yaliti to join them from the men's camp. There wasn't a blanket or one article of clothing between them. I had three blankets and a sleeping bag and needed them all. Little wonder, I thought, that their bodies were scarred with burns.

Our own small discomforts passed unnoticed when I considered their lot, although I must say I would rather not have had to put up with water from Jupiter Well. As the tanks on the vehicles emptied we replenished them from the well. To wash in it we used salt water soap. I'm convinced that soap would also have improved the taste, and certainly the smell. Thereafter, our coffee tasted like medicine, and tea like a double-dose. To the Pintubi, however, it was simply Kapi. To them, there is no such thing as bad water. It would need to be bad indeed not to sustain life; so long as it does that they are not concerned about the taste or the smell.

Our food was also becoming less varied as the tucker-boxes ran low. We finished the last tin of creamed rice, used as breakfast porridge, and the last fruit juice. Jeremy Long was obliged to start rationing so that we would have enough for the return journey.

Before leaving Haasts Bluff I cooked a sugarbag full of salt beef. This had been with us in the sun and dust for nine days but we were still eating it — as sliced cold beef, as curry and grit, as stew, and for one evening meal I used it as the base for fried rice. I'm afraid I cannot recommend it to Oriental cooks. There were 'left-overs', which didn't surprise me at all, but there wasn't much left within five minutes of its delivery to the Pintubi camp.

To make our ration position worse, we managed to spill a jerrycan of petrol in the tray of a truck. Much of our bagged food was lost, including a bag of sugar, half a bag of tea, and the remnants of my precious salt beef. That meant a further reduction in our rations for the run back to Papunya, which we expected to take several days.

Strong wind and dust made conditions trying, especially as neither had any effect in abating the nuisance caused by millions of flies. Jeremy Long undertook the distasteful duty of treating children affected by yaws. We were more than five hundred miles from the nearest medical aid, yet Dr Peter Dawes, sitting in an Alice Springs office, prescribed by wireless a treatment of cetrimide cream from the small stock of medicines we carried. On a subsequent patrol Long gave the children injections of penicillin.

If those with yaws were sick, it was as nothing compared with the violent illness of a small girl we took through the sandhills that morning for her first ride in a vehicle. Within a few miles she was overcome by motion sickness. She was red-eyed, shivering, and utterly miserable for the remainder of that day.

The wind and dust worried us for another reason. We continued our westerly drive, reaching a point almost six hundred miles from Alice Springs and closer to Wiluna in Western Australia. We were searching for the Jabangadi man, the husband of the three younger women at Jupiter Well, who was said to be hunting in the valleys formed by the sandhills north of our track. The little girl was his daughter, and she came with us in the hope that he would be found. But the wind and dust conspired against us: the wind by making smoke signals impossible, and the dust by erasing tracks. The deep imprint of our vehicle tyres made on the outward journey had been almost entirely obliterated when we returned an hour or so later. Finding fresh man-tracks in such conditions was made difficult even for our hawk-eyed professional trackers.

So Jabangadi the Stockman was allowed to remain in his desert hideout. Jeremy had tried in vain to make contact with him on earlier trips, but he is an elusive man. Why he should have come back to that desert with three wives and five children after the comparative security of the Canning stockroute was beyond my understanding.

In North Australia and on inland tribal grounds adjacent to adequate water the aborigines dance corroborees and hold religious ceremonies regularly. On some settlements they chant and dance every night, and are able to set dates weeks and even months ahead for great gatherings of the clans. A few of the big ritual ceremonies occupy months in their observance, notably the Kunapipi and Yabudarawa of eastern Arnhem Land, the Roper River and the East Kimberleys.

But in the desert it is difficult for tribesmen to come together in big groups, especially in times of drought. This does not, however, prevent them chanting song cycles, notably those belonging to the Kurangara cult, wherever two or three men are gathered together.

There is no evidence that big ritual ceremonies like Kunapipi have been held in the desert for many years. Perhaps, after heavy rains, it is possible that a messenger travels through the country, announcing to the isolated groups the time and place for a tribal meeting.

If so, the nomads would probably make it a season of religious observance, of chanting to pagan gods and totemic heroes, and a time for placating the spirits which guarantee the abundance of lizards and other basic foods.

Advantage may be taken of these infrequent opportunities to 'make' the young men in tribal initiations by ritual circumcision, an operation which would be performed with a stone knife — or perhaps with the untrained surgeon's teeth! That was the method commonly used in North Australia before European settlement and the introduction of sharp cutting implements. One of our gifts of mercy to the young tribesmen in areas which have contact with our society has been the razor blade. The Kurangara gathering can also be used as an opportunity for the settlement of grievances — though it is difficult to imagine how there could be any with such long distances between groups — and to promise young girls as wives to various young and old men. There may be a small exchange of trade goods, of artifacts, and of rare ochres brought in from their contacts with civilization by the eastern groups to the men of the west who had no cloth for pubic coverings and no red ochre for body decoration. In return they would take stone knives and wooden spears or their raw material — the barrel straight Acacia Nosepegii exclusive to the Gibson Desert.

This kind of inter-tribal trade has been going on in Australia for thousands of years, and from it there has developed a lingua franca — a trade-talk — between neighbouring tribes of differing tongues. In this way, artifacts made in Arnhem Land have eventually appeared more than a thousand miles away in South Australia, traded from tribe to tribe for many years, achieving simultaneously the reverse result that goods from the south came to Arnhem Land.

The Kurangara cult extends many hundreds of miles across the great central deserts. Tribesmen from the northern fringes in the south Kimberleys have been known to follow the mythical paths as far as the Nullarbor Plain, eight hundred miles away. Professor A. P. Elkin, one of Australia's leading authorities on the aborigines, refers to this common mythology as one of the greatest bonds between the community of tribes. In *The Australian Aborigines: How to Understand Them,* he tells of one myth concerning the emu and red ochre which is seven hundred miles long; that is, it is associated with natural features and localities along that length of territory. On one hand the 'ownership' of different sections of such a myth serves to distinguish tribes; on the other, as only one myth is concerned, each tribe is mutually dependent on all the others along this mythological path for its preservation. 'That is important,' he writes, 'for the welfare of man and nature is bound up with the myth and the rites in which it is re-enacted.'

Yaliti, aged sixty-five, may be thought to be a tired and frail man who would shirk the tribal duty of attending any ceremony which required him to walk hundreds of miles through the desert, having to keep himself fed and watered while he did so. But I would not be surprised if his regard for and observance of the ritual is stronger than that of men in whom it has been diluted by the waters of contact.

I saw one example of Yaliti's fervour as we were preparing to leave Jupiter Well. He was sitting around the campfire after lunch with Nosepeg and Jalyuri, still munching on his inevitable piece of damper. They may have been discussing a point of tribal law or ritual; whatever it was caused Yaliti to raise his voice above a whisper for the first time since we met him, and to make what appeared to me to be a clear-cut, even indignant statement. Having done that, he rose and pressed his penis firmly, in turn, into the right hands of both men. Four women and their children watched him do it. None of them took the slightest notice.

I don't know whether it was his equivalent of a handshake to seal a deal, a ritual act, or simply a farewell gesture. I did not like to ask.

The distinguished anthropologist, Mr M. J. Meggitt, of Sydney, in his book *Desert People,* which deals chiefly with the Wailbri tribe, a Pintubi neighbour, mentions two examples of penis-holding.

In one, a man publicly accused at a ceremonial gathering of a serious offence may try to place his penis in the hand of an actual or classificatory brother. If the latter permits this he undertakes to plead for the accused and, should the plea fail, to fight beside him.

In the other, Meggitt says that when men from another community or tribe arrive for a ceremony they usually first perform a penis-offering ritual with their hosts. Each visitor approaches each of the seated hosts in turn and lifts the latter's arm. He presses his penis against the host's hand so that the subincised urethra is in full contact with the palm, and then draws the penis firmly along the hand. A man with a grievance against a visitor refuses his hand for the ritual. At this sign of hostility, the visitor at once presents his penis to each of his classificatory brothers among the hosts. Should none of them take it, the outsider must be ready to fight or flee; he now knows that public opinion is solidly against him.

Yaliti, therefore, may have been doing nothing more than establishing that good relations existed between him and his visiting tribesmen, though neither Nosepeg nor Jalyuri were classificatory brothers—that is, belonging to the same 'skin' or subsection.

We were now ready to leave. Nosepeg, Jalyuri and Anatjari collected pituri for the trip and rolled it in corkwood ash. Apparently they like their cigarettes cork-tipped, too. Each would have his own supply of this mild narcotic, keeping it either in a piece of cloth or a quid behind the ear, according to the degree of his sophistication.

An hour before our departure, old Yaliti became garrulous — nothing to be compared with Nosepeg, of course, but, for him, quite talkative.

He muttered softly and continuously, no doubt regretting the loss so soon of his new-found wealth in food — the only kind of wealth that really matters to a nomad.

We gave them flour, tea and sugar. As a last request, the women asked for matches. These magic 'waru', or firesticks, had evidently made a greater impression on them, in terms of convenience, than anything else except a remarkable flame-throwing device used constantly by Frank Few. This was a conventional cigarette lighter, but they were fascinated by it. It is possible that they could begin to understand the burning wooden match-stick, although not what caused ignition when abrasive and inflammable substances were rubbed together. But a cigarette lighter which burst into flame on being opened was beyond them. Like most of the puzzles we had with us, they did not attempt a solution or show the slightest interest in what made them work.

The matches would gave them freedom for a few days from the necessity to carry firesticks whenever they moved, though I wondered who would be the first brave soul to strike one. While we were with them I did not see Yaliti or any of the women attempt to do so.

What would happen to these eleven people when we left? First, Yaliti was to make contact with the Jabangadi man, if possible, and bring him to a rendezvous with Jeremy Long a fortnight later at Likil waterhole forty miles to the east. (The Jabangadi was found on that second trip, but not because Yaliti brought him in.)

After that? They would go back from Jupiter Well into the sandhills whence they came, not because they would have any future fear of the apparitions driven by white men, but because that was where food was most plentiful, even though it consisted mainly of Mountain Devils and fungoid truffles. They would hunt there until the food was depleted or the waterhole dried up; then they would move on like the nomads they were, expecting nothing of the desert except that it should support them, however precariously. Yaliti may die there. One day soon, unless evacuated with his family, he may be caught between two drying waterholes and perish like dozens of other Pintubi before him, the head of a household who won't be home with dinner because the sandhills have claimed him at last. Having survived for so long, it is probable that he will die of old age, a fate that is comparatively rare in the Gibson Desert.

I shook hands with the old man. It was a gesture he did not understand and Nosepeg had to instruct him. In doing so, I felt a profound respect, even admiration, for him.

We were going away from him in four-wheel-drive vehicles with enough food, water and guides to take us safely back to a place where the means of survival was available for money, to a land of canteens, supermarkets, houses and pipe-lines.

But he had only his spears and his two feet. When the food we gave him was eaten he would become an independent man again, matching his wits against the desert, and its wild life, surviving as he and his forefathers had since they first crossed from the lush lands and dropped the curtain of sand behind them.

'Good hunting,' I said, and hoped that it would be so.

Among the aborigines the goodbyes were abrupt and in some cases were not said at all. As far as I could see, none of the Pintubi in our party said a word in farewell to the women and children of Yaliti's horde — nor had they been greeted on arrival.

The desert had taught them not to show emotion of any kind.

Yet their hearts at times must be full to overflowing, bursting with sentiment they cannot express.

I recall one unforgettable incident to substantiate this theory that their reticence is only skin-deep.

During our outward journey I asked Nosepeg whether the naked people we had seen didn't suffer miserably in the cold weather. He insisted that they did not.

'No blankets, no clothes — properly way!' he said. 'These people don't need them.'

But Nosepeg no longer had his good military overcoat. He had given it away, an almost priceless possession in his own life, so that the Jabangadi's daughter, the small girl who was ill, could be wrapped up and kept warm.

I asked him before we left if he wasn't going to reclaim it.

'No! Leave him!' he said, in a tone of voice which did not invite comment. And then, to change the subject: 'Give me cigarette.'

Nosepeg rather immodestly told me that he was Boss of all the Pintubi living at Papunya. My own observations confirmed that he was a man of considerable influence, but the title of 'Boss' is one that aborigines do not recognize. No adult male has the right to expect obedience from another.

With a twinkle in his eye, he said that his 'whitefeller' name was really John Carter, a corruption of Junkata, his tribal name. Anatjari was tentatively named Ridge Runner, after his magnificent crossing of the sandhills to find Yaliti. Inevitably, that will eventually be corrupted to Reg Runner, and the reason for it forgotten. The fourteen year old Jambajimba boy, Nim-Nim, we christened Sandy Groper as testimony of his discovery in Western Australia.

By whatever name Nosepeg is known in future, he will remain for me always as a delightful companion, a man who talked endlessly but with the saving grace of being worth listening to. I have often heard aborigines described, collectively, as lazy, generally by people who have had no experience of them or are employing them on starvation wages which give no incentive to work. I wonder how many white laborers would qualify as 'lazy' if asked to work for two or three pounds a week, and often less? But Nosepeg, whatever he was paid, cannot be put in that category. He is the most active and industrious aboriginal I have known. He was always in the vanguard of any search for spear trees, and in their conversion to spears. He was active in smoke-making and track identification, and was chief cook, story-teller and interpreter.

I ribbed him and he ribbed me unmercifully. Once, probably because he was searching the horizon for smoke, I saw tracks on the ground before him, and presented him with my spectacles. Thereafter he lost no opportunity in pointing to objects he knew I would not be able to see.

'You're proper blind,' he said.

His mirth and good fellowship were irrepressible. Rather than ask for a cigarette he would sometimes point to an empty packet and wait for my reaction. When I responded to such a slight hint he was delighted. He loved to communicate indirectly in this fashion, or by sign talk; but, when necessary, he was not backward in making his needs known.

Idleness of any kind irked him. He would rather walk than stand still. The days I spent in the bush with him were enchanting. He showed me wild honey, the holes of mice and goannas, and the tracks of many small animals, but he was shrewd enough to sprinkle his commentary with requests for gifts of clothing to be sent to him when I returned home. I thought his strangest wish — but one typical of his nature — was for a substance apparently available only in Darwin which makes playing cards slippery. The old gambler was setting his traps.

'I want to win big-mob money at Papunya,' he said.

That day he did me the honour of assigning me to the Jungarai skin group of the Pintubi tribe. Jeremy Long, whose Man Friday he is, belongs to the Juburula skin and is therefore Nosepeg's classificatory brother. I qualified only as a cousin.

To avoid misinterpretation, this should not be taken as bestowing the kind of blood-brothership nonsense claimed by others. Nosepeg was joking.

'You're my cousin,' he said. But he laughed. I'm not his cousin, and he knows it. I belong to the Australian skin of the European tribe.

Anatjari in the Big White Way

The value placed on water by the Pintubi nomads was impressed on my mind forever that day by Anatjari. In a natural and unrehearsed way he showed me his alternative to washing his greasy hands in water which, to any man of the desert, would constitute wanton waste. He simply scooped up a handful of red dirt and 'washed' them with that. It did not make them clean, but it did dry the grease.

At a camp near Wudungu, where we had first met him, Anatjari took silent leave of his two wives, his five year old son, and his two infant daughters. He was coming with us on his first excursion to The Big White Way at Papunya settlement, which might be compared roughly with the first visit of a country hayseed to a big city. Nim-Nim was coming, too.

The only member of the family to react in any way to this news was the small boy. He screamed, jumping up and down in a terrible tantrum at being left behind after the excitement of the ride to Jupiter Well . . . and the several days of damper-feasting that went with it.

Anatjari took no notice of him. We were already in the trucks and moving across the spinifex plain. In any case, I'm sure he saw the boy's mother pick up a waddy and threaten him with it. We would soon be out of sight, and he would forget quickly. Nevertheless, I thought it a splendid reversal of form for a boy who, only a few days earlier, had fled into the bush when told of our arrival.

For Anatjari and Nim-Nim this was to be the Great Adventure.

I hoped, for his own sake, that by the time we reached Papunya, Anatjari would have solved the riddle of the clothes he wore. He was still having trouble, and was as unable as a baby to dress himself in shirt and trousers. Nose-peg explained repeatedly that trousers were worn with the buttons in front . . . a simple enough matter but one which this man just could not grasp.

Before leaving the Stone Age behind, I thought it would be an exciting experience to accompany one of these nomads on a hunting expedition. I wanted to see how they found fresh goanna tracks and followed them to a hole in the ground. I hoped that we might be lucky enough to see a euro and stalk it. The idea was that I should hunt with Anat-jari while we walked towards Likilnga waterhole, where we would rejoin Jeremy Long with the vehicles.

Unfortunately, the hunting party wasn't confined to one man. Nosepeg, Jalyuri, Nim-Nim and Snowy joined us. Nomadic hunters do not operate in groups, which would multiply their chances of betrayal to the game they wished to kill. Anatjari lost interest immediately. Matters were not helped by the fact that we left the vehicles in a grove of Acacia Nosepegii. Nosepeg, Jalyuri and Anatjari were dis-tracted from the purpose of the exercise and went off to cut spears. When I tried to explain that this was a hunting party, I was silently dismissed as a madman. Nobody but a men-tally deficient person would hunt while plenty of flour, tea and sugar was available on the trucks.

It was impossible to convey to these men that I wanted to see them hunting . . . that I wanted to learn at first hand how they found food in a place where apparently none existed

. . . how they distinguished between old tracks and new tracks . . . I wanted, above all, to say that I had been hunting with a professional desert hunter and that we had caught *x* number of goannas.

What happened instead was that I had a long walk through spinifex and sand dunes with a bitterly cold wind blowing. To cap it all, Nosepeg helped to sabotage my plans but then pressed me into service as one of his spear-bearers after his own load of raw materials became too heavy. I was glad enough when we walked into the dinner-camp at Likilnga, with sore feet and buckling knees. And I was thankful that I didn't have to eat the harvest provided by our huntsmen, which was nil. One item only has been put down on the credit side of this experience: I now know very well what it feels like to be as hungry as a hunter.

Around the campfires that night the three aboriginal men sang tribal chants, and were delighted when Frank Few made a tape recording and played it back to them. Anatjari's introduction to electronic magic began in earnest when he heard his own voice singing to him . . . while his mouth remained closed. At first it wasn't closed at all, of course — it was wide open in wonder at this miraculous box which took his words from him, stored them in a manner he could not begin to understand, and then repeated them perfectly.

'Ahhhh!' he said. I knew what he meant, for he had said just that when he saw his first white face at Wudungu. It was obviously his equivalent of 'Well, I'll be blowed . . . "

Next day we 'planted' a drum of flour and a bag of barley in a bush beside the track. Nosepeg organized this, explaining that a group of three men, their wives and children were hunting in the area. He hoped they would find the cache, indicated in fifty thousand square miles of spinifex by nothing more than an arrow drawn on the ground with his foot by Jeremy Long.

The reality of the desert was apparent again at a place called Inindi. As usual, the name referred to a waterhole. It was fifteen feet deep, not more than three feet in diameter . . . and dry! A family had obviously lived there, digging deeper on a soak which yielded perhaps a gallon a day . . . until it disappeared altogether. Then they would have moved quickly to the next hole, a full day's walk away, hoping that when they reached it there would be enough to slake their raging thirsts.

The petrol and water we left at Sandy Blight Junction on the outward trip were still there. The tracks showed that no vehicle had been through the junction in the week we were west of there.

Jeremy estimated that one vehicle a month might pass that way between April and October. In summer, all traffic would cease. Fortunately the sandhills ran unfailingly from east to west . . . and I saw four hundred miles of them. If they ran north and south we would not have been there at all.

By this time our vehicles had become bristling weapon carriers. Nosepeg, Jalyuri and Anatjari, working every night of our stay in the desert, now had sixty-four spears strapped to the roofs and sides of the trucks.

I asked Nosepeg what he intended doing with them all.

'Might sell'im,' he said. 'Plenty tourists want to buy.'

It is not an exaggeration to say that the changes which began for Anatjari and Nim-Nim as we approached Papunya were world-shattering . . . their understanding of the world they lived in was shattered completely. The desert world . . . the Stone Age world in which their ancestors had lived since the Time of Dream gradually disintegrated as they made new and ever more remarkable discoveries.

The very beliefs on which their lives were based would have to be adjusted . . . for nothing would ever be the same again.

They would see at close hand the aeroplanes that flew over their tribal land; they would see mechanical contraptions like the road grader which had ploughed through the desert; but the beginnings of their new conception of life were to be mercifully simple.

The first episode occurred as we drove into mulga scrub west of Mt Liebig, about two hundred miles from Alice Springs. We were back in the land of the big red kangaroo . . . which long ago forsook the Gibson Desert as a place fit only for human beings — the Pintubi. In hundreds of miles of spinifex and sandhills we had not seen more than two animals bigger than dingoes. They were euros, small kangaroos which somehow managed to survive where their big red brothers could not. But natural camouflage in the desert is so sparse that even the wily Pintubi hunters seldom spear one. They do their best, crawling slowly and painfully towards a euro by using the pointed spinifex as cover. It is not often, therefore, that euro meat is on the Pintubi menus. In the camps I saw there was no evidence of one having been eaten.

When we saw our first big reds Anatjari and Nim-Nim were amazed, not only by their size but by their numbers. Yet their astonishment was just beginning.

Jeremy Long aimed a rifle at the kangaroo nearest to him. There was an expectant hush from the sophisticated members of the party who knew what to expect — in fact, their salivary glands were already working, for we had been without fresh meat for a long time.

But Anatjari and Nim-Nim had never seen a rifle fired. They had no idea what would happen and, when the kangaroo was shot, even less conception of what had caused its death.

Anatjari was a man who hunted game with spears, and had done so all his life. When he threw one he could follow its flight either until it missed or transfixed the animal. He was completely dumbfounded by this magic: a man pointed something he did not understand at a kangaroo, there followed an explosion, and the kangaroo's death was caused at long range by something that couldn't be seen!

How do you explain such phenomena to a man who has never heard of gunpowder and has never seen a bullet?

I asked Nosepeg what Anatjari would think had killed the kangaroo.

'It's proper magic to him,' he said. 'He thinks might-be there is a doctor-feller in that rifle.'

I translated this as meaning that the rifle contained a spirit which could communicate with the kangaroo in such a way that the animal was suddenly stricken, grabbed its body with its paws, jumped a few feet, and fell down dead.

Perhaps it was for this reason that many aborigines believe that a rifle can kill at unlimited ranges. Even Nosepeg, who should have known better, tried to shoot them when they were too far away. Then he would spit in disgust and say, 'Rifle rubbish! Boomerang more better.'

The instinct of a hunter when an animal is hit and wounded by a spear is to run after it. Anatjari, beside himself with joy, began running towards the kangaroo Long had shot. He realized half way that running probably wasn't necessary, so he stopped and uncharacteristically slapped me on the back with a delighted chuckle. He was in a frenzy of excitement and, if possible, that was doubled when a second kangaroo was shot. He had no idea what was inside our tucker boxes, or whether there was enough flour for another damper. But he understood the message of two dead kangaroos: a full belly. He could scarcely wait for us to reach the night-camp, and a banquet extraordinary.

The second simple episode occurred a few miles further on when we overtook a white mechanic, Tom Bevan, and three aborigines. They were towing our abandoned third vehicle back to Papunya.

Jalyuri, who had been in civilization for a few weeks, was quite at home and mixed freely with these strangers. Anatjari, however, stayed in the background and Nim-Nim got behind a truck where he couldn't be easily seen.

I had imagined that aborigines would be at home among their own folk wherever they found them. That is not so. These desert men were strangers among strangers just as surely as if they had been Laplanders in Tibet.

The third episode happened with cattle at Warren Creek bore, where we camped for the night. I suppose I had taken it for granted that every person living in Australia in 1963 would have seen cattle, but here were two who hadn't. Earlier in the day I pointed out the track of a bullock to Anatjari and was puzzled when he turned away.

I mentioned this to Nosepeg, who said: 'That man has never seen a bullock's track before. He's frightened.'

On Nim-Nim's face there had been a look of utter mystification. Tracks were the things he understood best of all, yet here was something he could not understand and I could not explain.

At the bore, where cattle had come in to water, there were hundreds of such tracks. I could see that Anatjari did not

like the idea of camping there. His eyes moved with per-
plexity from one group of tracks to the next. He may have
been experiencing sensations similar to those of the Sherpas
who first found tracks in the Himalayas of what has become
known as The Abominable Snow Man.

Eventually Anatjari and Nim-Nim must have become
accustomed to them, or been reassured by Jalyuri and Nosepeg, although they could still only guess at the size and
shape of the wild beasts that made them. They walked
across them to a trough and a five thousand gallon squatters'
tank — the first artificial means of storing water they had
seen. Anatjari climbed on a drum to look inside the tank and
was obviously astonished. The only water he had seen in his
life had come from desert soaks and rockholes. But here in a
circular tank of iron — the biggest single 'thing' of his experience — was water seven feet deep which flowed out as
required into troughs so that people might drink.

People? How could I explain to him that this water . . .
this ocean of it pumped from the ground by a machine . . .
was not for man at all, but for his animals?

Anatjari and Nim-Nim, at that stage, had seen nothing
more of civilization than this squatters' tank, the pump, and
the troughs, but were already confused. That confusion was
soon to be compounded.

Just before dusk a number of cows and calves walked in
slowly to drink at the trough. As they appeared through the
mulga and long grass Jeremy Long pointed to them and
shouted: 'Bullocky!'

Anatjari and Nim-Nim sprang to their feet, but remained
crouching in the instinctively alert attitude of hunting men.

Fortunately we were between them and the cattle, and
Nosepeg and Jalyuri were in the camp to reassure them.
Otherwise it is possible that they may have run away, for
these were the biggest living things they had seen. They

crouched for a long time, never taking their eyes from these animal Martians.

Nosepeg said later that both the man and the youth were trembling with fright, and had to be told repeatedly that there was no danger.

'They got pimple-along-skin-like-goose,' he said.

I wouldn't be surprised if they had a restless night, although next day they were even more astonished when they saw horses which galloped parallel with the vehicles, their tails and manes flying in the clouds of dust raised by their hoofs. These were monsters indeed.

At Mt Liebig that night, with bullocks in attendance, I thought, 'Well, we are back in civilization . . . back in the land of the white man and all his works.' In my wanderings around North and Central Australia I have often referred to localities as 'The Outback'. But I knew that, henceforth, these other corners would never again hold for me the significance of outback remoteness that they had in the past.

For me, the outback would now always be west of Mt Liebig, west of the Kintore Ranges, west of Mt Liesler and Mt Webb in the land of the Pintubi nomads.

The two kangaroos that Long had shot were baked in the coals and hot sand, their legs protruding grotesquely. After an hour or so the blackened, fur-charred carcasses were cut up by Nosepeg, Jalyuri and Anatjari, and the meat was divided between them.

For Anatjari this was a comparatively easy task, for he used a sharp hunting knife made of steel. In the past, he had had to cut his meat, when he had any, with blunt knives of stone.

The division wasn't quite as arbitrary as it might have been if the kangaroos had been speared by one of these men. But the shots had been fired by Long, Nosepeg's 'brother' of the Juburula skin. Nosepeg, whether entitled to it or not, therefore had first choice.

Thereafter, the division was strictly on the basis of 'One, one and one', as Nosepeg put it. One great haunch to each man and one left over. I don't know what happened to that — perhaps Snowy Jambajimba was given a hand-out. There was fair division of ribs, liver, kidneys, hearts, heads, tails and breastmeat. 'Soft' meat, such as the liver, is normally reserved for the old men of the tribe whose teeth have seen better days.

The kangaroos had been gutted and cooked with the fur on. The meat was still half-raw when divided, with blood oozing from it. Nosepeg indicated that he liked his meat well done, or his displeasure with the cook, by throwing a piece in the coals for further cooking. Anatjari appeared not to mind: he tore at a great haunch with his strong teeth and allowed the blood to drip unchecked into his beard. He ate as though he had never eaten in his life before, whereas he had done almost nothing else for a week. Nim-Nim was hungry, too; the fright the bullocks gave them certainly had not affected their appetites.

When they finished eating, the 'left-overs' were hung in the forks of mulga trees, to remain there away from the ants while they slept deeply with full bellies. Eating would be resumed at daylight and the balance taken into Papunya as the nucleus of the 'household' larders they would have to establish. Normally they would have carried it on their heads, or wrapped in a swag or a blanket . . . but the modern world had caught up with them in many ways, and these prime steaks, roasts, and cutlets were placed in a plastic bag provided by Frank Few.

At dawn we were under attack.

The air around us whistled with bone-tipped spears, less than fifty miles from our base at Papunya.

We had penetrated two hundred miles beyond the Western Australian border, through country where nature was hostile even if the natives were friendly, without being exposed to danger more serious than being stranded in broken-down vehicles.

Yet now, so close to home, we were attacked. The dawn came sibilantly, the great hiss of a multiple barrage of spears cleaving the air. I pulled my head in literally, cowering beneath the blankets, expecting any moment that I might be transfixed.

The spears were the beaks of a million grey, blue and red parrots which flew in flocks at incredible speed over our camp to the water trough beyond. They strafed the camp site at grass-top level, skimming past my swag with so little to spare that I might have reached up and caught one — or had my hand pierced. Their wings whirred in the melody of multitude. I had never seen so many birds in one place at one time. It was unbelievable that they could fly in huge flocks at such electric speed without crashing madly into one another, yet there was nothing to suggest that wingtips ever touched. In the desert we had seen a few small hawks and occasional flocks of small finches near waterholes. But Anatjari and Nim-Nim were learning that they were entering the world of Bigger-and-Better in birdlife as well as material things.

Later, when I approached the troughs to shave and wash, the birds took off in uncountable thousands. The beat of their wings was like an Indian war cry, like a prelude of woodwinds to a cyclonic concerto.

Nosepeg the Irrepressible also shaved for his arrival home

at Papunya — with a razor blade but no razor. Then he helped prepare Anatjari for his debut . . . not into society, but into civilization itself.

His beard was trimmed, his hair was combed, and he wore a white band of cloth around it.

The centre of his forehead was then adorned with a broad black band of charcoal mixed with kangaroo fat . . . black superimposed on black, the band running from the hairline to the bridge of his nose. Jalyuri was similarly decorated.

They were badges of identification. The other Pintubi and Wailbri tribesmen at Papunya would know when they saw these marks that Anatjari and Jalyuri were from the desert . . . from the sand-country west of the border . . . authentic primitives even to people who were themselves only a few years removed from nomadism. The badges were tribal passports; the tribesmen who saw them knew that help and safe-conduct for these men were expected from the remainder of the aboriginal community.

Anatjari wore his shirt and trousers and, outwardly, looked like any other Central Australian aboriginal. If I had seen him at Papunya on my way to the west I could never have guessed that only a few days earlier he had not seen a white face or tasted food cooked with flour.

Jalyuri, inevitably, wore the navy blue coat of a discarded lounge suit that had been on his back almost constantly since our departure. His hair was combed and bound, his red corded band was around his forehead, his smile was in place and his teeth gleamed — but the coat made him look like a tramp. A warm tramp, to be sure, but a tramp never-theless.

Nim-Nim, or Sandy Groper, wore a shirt and shorts several sizes too large for him. I suspect they were a gift from

Jeremy Long, who is six feet five inches tall. They admitted a little more air than was strictly necessary, but at least he looked respectable.

Nosepeg looked like a gentleman, especially when standing next to me, because I hadn't shaved during the entire journey. My clothes, caked in red dust, stood waiting for me to get into them.

Then the trucks began to move . . . and I tried again, vainly perhaps, to put myself in Anatjari's clothes, to think as he must be thinking . . . I was twelve years old, a bush boy from the country in Victoria who had never seen a big city, and I was being taken to Melbourne for my first visit. I remembered the express train racing in from Ballarat, Horsham and points west and I saw the huge metropolis — trams, automatic lifts, buildings ten storeys tall, Luna Park, the zoo, a theatre where stars twinkled in the ceiling, a tiled swimming pool, and thousands of acres of streets and houses where I was hopelessly lost. Well, I knew a little of what Anatjari and Nim-Nim must be feeling . . .

And then the Papunya settlement came into view. First we saw the galvanized iron roofs and elevated tanks and poles carrying power lines. Anatjari and Nim-Nim began quaking with fear.

Anatjari sat on the back of the truck and held on to supporting bars with both hands . . . and let his knees knock.

When our truck had stopped I pointed this out to Nosepeg. 'Poor bugger,' he said. 'Too many houses, too many people. He's got proper fright.'

Nim-Nim was struck dumb.

Their eyes were never still, roving constantly while they clung desperately to their steel supports, perhaps searching for the expression they couldn't see in the sightless eyes of all the buildings — the glass windows which stared unblinkingly at them from apparitions which did not appear to live.

Hundreds of other aborigines milled around the trucks or remained in the distance, all of them fully clothed, all well-nourished, but all strangers — this Anatjari would have seen at a glance, and wondered where they got their food . . . for none of them had spears or goannas hanging from their belts.

And then these unbelievable buildings, immense things twenty feet high and one hundred feet long, with doors that opened and closed as people went in and out . . .

. . . and the canteen, with its wondrous display of clothing and food, bags of flour in stacks up to the ceiling, shelves full of tins and bottles that he knew contained meat and other food . . .

. . . and the conventional motor cars, sedans with windows which wound up and down, and a lid at the rear which opened when a man wanted to put something inside . . .

. . . and, oh! how clean they seemed, white women with white children, their hair so fine and blonde, their eyes blue — a colour he had not seen in human eyes. The women had red fingernails and red lips and wore high-heeled shoes and spoke to their menfolk before being spoken to . . . quite harshly it seemed . . . in a way that would instantly have earned them a thrashing in the desert . . .

. . . and the tractors drawing trailers loaded with firewood and drums of refuse and roaring as though they were more important than the sedan cars . . .

. . . and what were those strings threaded through bits of wood planted in the ground? Fences? What were fences? To keep some people in and other people out. To a man whose only fence, throughout his life, had been the horizon, that was incomprehensible.

I could see that Anatjari and Nim-Nim felt strange and miserable among these strange black and white people and the incredible works of man. I wondered how they may have reacted if, instead of Papunya settlement, their first view of the Big White Way had been The Town That is Alice — that enormous place of five thousand people on the banks of the Todd River only one hundred and fifty miles away. One day soon, perhaps, they would see it, and be frightened again. But what if they had been picked up in helicopters and dropped into civilization in Melbourne or Sydney? They may not have survived the shock.

In a little while, when they had absorbed it all, we drove them out to the Pintubi camp on the outskirts of the settlement, where there were other, smaller houses, modest shelters which did not frighten them.

Jalyuri led them through the throng of tribesmen who mobbed our vehicles . . . to a new plot of ground behind a stunted bush. There they sat, waiting for the world to start moving again.

Anatjari would soon be taken back to the desert by Jeremy Long, but he would have a week to accustom himself to the new life. I wondered if he would remain out there. Would the tastes he had acquired for flour, tea and sugar be so strong that they would draw him back with his wives and son and daughters? I think he cast a vote for Papunya after lunch when we took him to the canteen, to the inside of one of those monstrous buildings. He had been paid for several spears he made, paid with paper he probably thought was useless. But now, with Nosepeg instructing him, he bought a packet of sugar . . . at least, that is what Nosepeg said was inside the paper . . . and a packet of tea, and a tin of bully beef, and a shirt . . . all of this treasure for that single bit of worthless-seeming green paper.

And then I thought, 'Well, that's the start. Now he has the flavour of a canteen he'll want to come back.'

The desert would lose one of its adornments, a man of stature who knew it, a man who had studied its tantrums and learned to respect its treachery . . . a man who could confidently take his horde away from one water when the game around it had been hunted out . . . away to the next water, wherever that was, by the only means they had ever known — on foot. And when they got there the waterhole might be dry and, thirsting, they would have to walk again, through the night, so that they might arrive, perishing, at the next hole . . .

What a pity if such a man should leave the desert. And yet the alternative was unacceptable, for it meant the inevitable disappearance from the world they were just entering of the few Stone Age men remaining on earth.

Epilogue

Jeremy Long went back to Jupiter Well, and returned Anatjari to his country.

He made further excursions south of our track. Near
Pollock Hills he found a young girl, aged about six, sitting
alone in the desert. She was holding two dingo puppies she
wanted as pets. The puppies' mother was howling miserably
in the hills beyond.

Presently an even smaller girl, aged only three, walked
in alone from a waterhole four hundred yards away. She
carried water in a tin on her head.

The elder girl was garrulous and talked constantly; the
younger was nervous and often hid behind her half-sister.
Her mother had died a year earlier.

Two hours later the mother of the first girl and a sister
aged about thirteen arrived. They had been hunting and had
found several lizards. Later still, the father, Kuku, came in
with a crown of lizards in his hair. They had been seen by
Long on his patrol in the previous year.

Jeremy also made contact at Likilnga with Kulaya, the
Jabangadi man who had the reputation of being a stockman,
and has been referred to throughout these pages as such.

But that was shown to be a fable, and proved to me again
the desirability of not putting too much credence on information gained through interpreters. Jeremy discovered that
Kulaya had never worked on the Canning stockroute, as has
been stated. He claimed, in fact, that he had never seen

white people. The story about his ability as a stockman
began on the day near Pollock Hills when the tribesmen saw
three bullocks which suddenly appeared in their country.
The Pollock Hills are two hundred miles east of the stockroute, but they had come from there after rain, existing on
the water-filled parakelia. In this way, other bullocks are
known to have crossed the desert to Haast Bluff, Mount
Doreen and Curtin Springs.

Most of the tribesmen were terrified of the bullocks. They
had never seen anything like them. Kulaya may have been
afraid, too, but he was a man of great courage . . . and he was
hungry. He led the others on a marauding expedition. With
broad wooden-bladed spears, they chased the bullocks . . .
and chased them . . . and chased them until they could run
no longer. Then they killed them, in a bloody life-and-death
struggle that can only be imagined. Each of the animals
weighed about one thousand pounds. The tribesmen feasted
for weeks on the flesh.

Kulaya had apparently learnt the art of killing cattle while
hunting with people who lived nearer the stockroute and
often harassed drovers taking big mobs from the Kimberleys
to Wiluna. If that was so, they were fortunate that the
western fringe of the desert was so sparsely settled by Europeans. Similar episodes on the eastern fringe led to punitive
expeditions and massacres.

Since writing the account of my own brief expedition into
the Pintubi country I have read Ernest Giles' journal of his
1874 and 1876 expeditions. I have also read *Spinifex and
Sand*, written by the Hon. David Carnegie and published
in London in 1898 — two years after Carnegie and three
companions crossed from Coolgardie on the southern gold-
fields of Western Australia to Hall's Creek in the Kimberleys,

and then returned by way of Lake MacDonald — the country we entered sixty-seven years later.

Both accounts made me feel very humble. Giles and Carnegie were beset by what would now seem insuperable difficulties. Whereas in this story I have probably dramatised situations which needed no such embellishment, Carnegie and Giles spoke about their exploits almost as though they happened every day — although Carnegie never tired of speaking in highly disparaging terms about the desert. Having been there, I found no difficulty in agreeing with him.

Spinifex and Sand contains some graphic descriptions of Carnegie's meetings with the Pintubi, and he was remembered: at Jupiter Well the old man named Yaliti told us his father had been one of a group of tribesmen who saw Carnegie. Perhaps he was a man Carnegie admitted chaining to a tree to secure him. Perhaps his wife was the old woman Carnegie tied to his camel saddle and fed on salty beef until she was forced to lead him to water.

Carnegie equipped his expedition with nine camels which cost seventy-two pounds each. When that sum is related to the present day value of the pound, it will be seen that he was paying for a camel almost as much as one now pays for a small car. His equipment, which he listed in great detail, included nosepegs, cord for noselines, long needles for mending saddles, kerosene (to check vermin), tar for mange in camels, picks, shovels, axes, solder for mending water casks, seven lbs of Epsom salts, six bottles of embrocation, three bottles of carbolic oil, revolvers, shotguns, rifles, a bicycle lamp for night observation, (we had electric light!), compasses, telescopes, 700 lbs of flour, 420 lbs of tinned meat, 60 lbs of tinned fish (not fit for human consumption and thrown away), 200 lbs rice, 70 lbs oatmeal, 100 tins baking soda, 50 tins jam, 140 lbs of sugar, 40 lbs of salt, 30 lbs of tea, 50 lbs of tobacco, 100 lbs of preserved potatoes, 4 bottles of good brandy, 1 bottle of rum, 1 hair clipper.

These stores, and many others, were calculated to last six months. It was all packed in large leather bags. When the expedition started each camel had an average load of 530 lbs, but two had loads of 750 lbs.

Carnegie made it quite clear that the brandy was for medicinal purposes only. 'Even if we had been able to afford the room I should not have carried more. For I am convinced that in the bush a man can keep his health better, and do more work, when he leaves liquor entirely alone,' he wrote.

Carnegie describes the desert he entered on August 22, 1896, thus:

'In the cheerless, waterless region around 26 to 22 degrees South latitude and 124 and 125 degrees East longitude, we saw no lakes, creeks or mountains, nor hills even prominent enough to deserve the name. Day after day we travelled over open treeless expanses covered only by the never-ending spinifex.

'As for animal life — well, one forgets that life exists until occasionally reminded of the fact by a bounding spinifex rat frightened from its nest. We tried to shoot them but counted it an unnecessary labour. Their small numbers would hardly have made it worthwhile to burden oneself with a gun. To see a dozen in a day was uncommon.'

There is an intriguing enigma in this quotation which Carnegie does not clarify. Were they shooting at the rats for sport, or were they, like the aborigines, proposing to eat them?

Although he travelled with far less comfort and at much

greater risk, many of Carnegie's experiences were almost identical with our own. For instance:

'On our first day in the desert we saw several smokes. They might be native signals, or simply fires for the purpose of burning off old spinifex to allow young feed to grow and thus attract rats. Or it might be that they were burning the country to hunt out the rats and lizards.

'On the 25th several old native camps put us on the alert, and presently we found a well — a shallow hole seven feet deep and two feet in diameter, entirely surrounded by high spinifex. Why there should even be water there, or how the blacks got to know of it, was a problem we could only guess at. Everything was so parched that we weren't surprised to find the well waterless.'

On my first day in the desert we also found a waterless well, and on other days we saw smokes which did not lead us to natives.

At one stage Carnegie's reserve of water was low to the point of desperation. He split his party in two so that simultaneous searches could be made in different directions, but they had still not found water on regrouping. They followed birds and dingo tracks hoping they would lead to water, but without luck.

'It was aggravating to be certain that water existed and yet be unable to find it,' Carnegie wrote.

They eventually crossed the tracks of a native man and his wife and followed them through all their deviations. They were able to identify tracks which showed where they had dug rats from holes and chased a lizard. Finally they reached the aborigines' camp. Several implements lay about, including a coolamon stained with damp clay. That meant there must be water nearby, and soon they were led by sparrows to a tiny well hidden in the spinifex — so perfectly hidden that they had passed within a few paces of it half an hour earlier. And there was water!

When I wanted a drink in this desert I took it from the tanks on our trucks. But for Carnegie it was a vastly different matter. After his initial supply was exhausted he had to find it, and when they did it often involved hours of work for him and his men scooping out the sand until they had water flowing into a well. The camels had to be tied down and watered in turn. After one long dry spell Carnegie was surprised to notice that his camels did not drink more than about two gallons each. But then he realized they had been living for several days on the parakelia I have described.

It was in country such as this, a hundred miles or so to the south, that Giles' companion, Alfred Gibson, disappeared without trace in 1874 and gave his name to his own vast grave: The Gibson Desert.

Giles, with Tietkins, Gibson and Andrews, left the Overland Telegraph Line in Central Australia that year in an attempt to penetrate as far as possible to the west.

They found the Rawlinson Ranges, where water was plentiful, and a depot camp established. Giles and Gibson then made a flying trip to the westward. The furthest point was reached on April 23, 1874, and from there the Alfred and Marie Range was visible.

At this point Gibson's horse broke down and soon died. Giles thereupon gave up his own horse and sent his companion back to the depot for relief. It was clear that Giles's horse could support only one of them. He who did so, by hurrying on, could return and save his companion. With a wave of his hat, Gibson shouted goodbye to his generous leader and rode off. He was never seen again. He failed to back the outgoing tracks, got lost in the night, became hopelessly bushed, and perished alone in the desert. Giles meanwhile struggled back on foot, every hour expecting relief which never came. At last, almost dead, he staggered into the depot camp.

A search was made for Gibson. The horse's tracks were followed for four days, but then had to be abandoned for fear that the remaining horses would perish. When last seen, his tracks were leading in the opposite direction from the depot camp, and seventy miles from it.

Giles must have had the taste of his friend's death in his mouth when he wrote: 'The country rolls along in ceaseless undulations of sand and ever-abounding spinifex. The region is so desolate that it is horrifying even to describe. The eye of God would have seen our solitary caravan as the only living objects, and must have contemplated our appearance with pitying admiration.'

It was country like this that Carnegie entered at great personal risk twenty-two years later. It was the same exactly when we entered it eighty-nine years after Giles — at no risk at all. We had adequate communications.

At a rockhole near McPherson's Pillar, Carnegie found water which he described thus: 'We got about two gallons of filth from it. I have swallowed all kinds of water in my time, but this was really too powerful. Had we been hard pressed it would undoubtedly have been used, but since we had not long left water we discarded this mixture after trying it on one of the camels, whose indignation was great.'

At that stage Carnegie recorded in his diary: 'Surely the most God-forsaken country on the face of the earth.'

True enough. I agree entirely. But the Pintubi have survived in it from that day to this.

Later Carnegie found an aboriginal camp and described it. I would say that it had not altered in one particular from the camps we saw sixty-seven years after him: a windbreak of spinifex and bushes, sleeping hollows scraped out of the sand, and several heaps of ashes indicating fires to keep the tribesmen warm. There were spears and yam sticks, a coolamon or two, and seeds used as food.

Soon afterwards Carnegie found the tracks of seven aborigines and gave chase. They were terrified and ran off at top speed. The natives disappeared — all except one.

'I overtook this figure on my camel and found it to be an old and hideous gin,' Carnegie wrote. 'Poor thing. She had stopped behind to pick up some dingo puppies. We needed water badly so, sorry as I was to be rude to a lady, I had to make her prisoner until she led us to it. That was not achieved without a great deal of trouble. She scratched, bit, spat, and tore at me with her horrid long nails and using, I felt sure, the worst language that her tongue could command.

'I had to carry this unsavoury object back to her camp, she clutching at every bush we passed when her hands were not engaged in clawing and scratching me. After her anger had somewhat abated she pointed out a rockhole from which they got water. I secured her with a light rope and descended the rockhole to see what supply was there. A little water was visible which I quickly baled into canvas bags. The bottom of the hole was filled in with dead sticks, leaves, the rotting bodies of birds and lizards, bones of rats and dingoes.'

This water they drank. And to think that I was critical of the supply at Jupiter Well, which Carnegie would have regarded as nectar!

On September 15, Carnegie and his party came upon another group of Pintubi people. He wrote:

'We came upon a party who were out hunting. They were unsuspicious of our presence until we were within a hundred yards of them. No words can describe the looks of terror and amazement on their faces when they saw us.

'Spellbound, they crouched in the black and smouldering ashes of the spinifex, mouths open and eyes staring, and then with one terrific yell they ran away. They kept up a ceaseless screaming, reminding me of a monkey-house at the zoo. Never by any possibility could they have seen camels or white men before. Their trembling fear was painful to see. They ran behind a tree and tried to hide there, but we caught up with them. Their incoherent yelling gradually died down to an occasional gulp. We made soothing sounds and patted their breasts and our own in turn, in sign of friendship. They were all terribly thin and diseased. We showed them by signs they readily understood that we had pressing need of water. When their fear subsided they led us to a well, and there we were joined by other members of the tribe. They were dressed in the fashionable desert costume of nothing at all. One man had a grass belt around his waist and from this there hung the spoils of his hunt — goannas and lizards. His gin followed with a further supply of reptiles and rats. The rats were plucked (they do not skin the animal, but pluck the hair as we do the feathers of a chicken), thrown in the fire and then greedily devoured, red and bloody, barely warm.

'They were strange primitive people, and yet kind and grateful. We anointed a sick man's wounds with tar and oil (a mixture used for mange in camels) and were rewarded by dog-like gratitude. The stillness of the night was broken only by the cry of a baby, and that was immediately suppressed by the mother biting its ear.'

Soon after leaving Family Well, a place we thought to be near Jupiter Well, Carnegie described the country again:
'Most wretched sand-ridge country. Absolutely no feed

for camels or any other animal. Such miserable country beggars description. Nothing is more heart-rending than to be forced to camp night after night with the knowledge that one's poor animals are wandering vainly in search of food. How anxiously each ridge was scanned when camping-time drew near. No feed. So on again another ridge or two. No feed, is again the cry. Just one more ridge. Still no feed. So we camped without it, and the famished camels wandered at night when they should have rested.'

Carnegie was thirteen months on the trip from Coolgardie to Hall's Creek and return. He had only his camels, his horses, his three assistants, and his wits to get him through.

We had motor vehicles and a wireless transceiver which would bring us quick rescue if we broke down.

He had to be constantly on the alert against attack by the Pintubi, who did not really appreciate the intrusion of their tribal land and the use of their water.

We had no such concern. On the contrary, we were welcomed because we took food to the natives.

Having been through the Gibson Desert in comparative comfort, I must acknowledge that Carnegie and his companions were valorous men.

And let it be remembered that Ernest Giles, Tietkins, Gibson and Andrews were there twenty years earlier.

As the men who first made the colour of our skin known to the desert people, they were worthy emissaries.

But I wonder if the Pintubi weren't more impressed by the incompetence they sometimes showed in living in the desert. For white men, the desert presented a constant threat to life, and they were glad to escape from it. To the Pintubi, it was their natural environment, although they were also required to treat it with respect.

The Gibson Desert today, apart from the track winding

from east to west through the sandhills, is just as it was a century ago . . . a millennium ago.

The people haven't changed, either. They are the same naked nomads that Giles and Carnegie knew.